Welcome to Britain

General thoughts'.

Welcome to Britain
An Anthology of Poems and Short Fiction

Edited by Ambrose Musiyiwa

Introduced by Regularise founder, Munya Radzi

Civic  Leicester

First published in Great Britain in 2023 by
CivicLeicester
y. https://www.youtube.com/user/CivicLeicester
f. https://www.facebook.com/CivicLeicester
CivicLeicester@gmail.com

ISBN-13: 978-1-9164593-8-0

Dedicated to all who are working to make Britain
a country that acknowledges the humanity of all people
and which treats everyone with decency, dignity and respect, and
to community activist, Jan Wild-Grant (1955-2022).

Contents

vii

Introduction

Welcome to Britain: An Anthology of Poems and Short Fiction is a timely publication that, among other things, sheds light on the ongoing contradictions of Britain's immigration policies, human rights approach, and its colonial legacy. With the recent death of Queen Elizabeth II and the accession of King Charles III, the country continues to grapple with its history of imperialism and racism, which is reflected in the mistreatment of migrants and people seeking asylum, particularly those from regions of the world that were subjected to British colonisation and invasion.

Despite welcoming Ukrainian refugees, the current government, led by Prime Minister Rishi Sunak and Home Secretary Suella Braverman, is continuing the anti-migrant stance of successive governments and is pushing through legislation that criminalises, punishes, and denies refuge to those who have little choice but to take desperate journeys to reach the UK, arriving through irregularised means. Consequently, many African and Asian migrants and refugees, instead of having their asylum claims processed promptly, are being warehoused in hotels and are denied basic rights, such as being able to work. Moreover, the government plans to intern people on barges, abandoned ferries and military barracks before shipping them off to Rwanda, which has been criticised as a violation of human rights.

At the heart of *Welcome to Britain* is recognition that the myths and fictions Britain likes to tell about itself need to be contested and subverted. Too often, the stories we are told about our history and our place in the world are incomplete, inaccurate, or even fabricated, perpetuating a cycle of prejudice, ignorance and injustice. By providing space for writers to offer - and for readers to encounter - counter-narratives, this anthology, among other things, draws attention to how Britain's history is inextricably linked to the global system of white supremacy, colonialism, slavery, and exploitation that has been in place over the past 500 years.

For centuries, England's and then Britain's empire expanded across the world, extracting resources, usurping lands, subjugating people, and exploiting labour for the benefit of its elite and the state, including its welfare system. The human toll of this global system is incalculable: tens of millions of lives have been lost or destroyed, families torn apart, cultures erased or suppressed, and vast territories stolen and despoiled. The legacy of this imperialism is still felt in many parts of the world today in the form of ongoing economic instability, political turmoil, and more.

While the explicit form of direct colonialism may have ended, its structures persist in many ways, including systemic racism, economic subjugation, and political interference. The wounds of the past continue to fester in the present, and European settler colonialism and neo-colonialism persist. The call for submissions for *Welcome to Britain* acknowledged these ongoing issues and sought to create space for them to be explored through the powerful and potentially transformative lens of poetry and short fiction.

In addition to offering accounts of daily life in Britain, the anthology encourages readers and writers alike to engage with the country's broader colonial legacies, which include the exploitation and subjugation of people in other parts of the world including Africa, Asia, the Caribbean, North and South America, Oceania and Ireland, and in this way contributes to discussion on how we create a more just and equitable world.

The call for submissions that led to the anthology also specifically acknowledged the need for reparations for the immense harm caused by Britain's involvement in the subjugation and enslavement of African people through chattel slavery and the slave trade. By exploring these issues, *Welcome to Britain* raises awareness on the ongoing impact of slavery and its aftermath on African/African-Caribbean/Black communities in Britain and beyond. It encourages readers and writers alike to examine the issues, ideological narratives, histories, lives, and demands that shape contemporary Britain, and offers a diverse range of perspectives on racial justice, the Black Lives Matter movement, human migration, refugee issues, the country's role in the world, responses to the conflict in Ukraine, and more. And it offers a unique opportunity for readers and writers to explore the multifaceted issues that shape contemporary Britain.

By amplifying diverse voices from around the world, *Welcome to Britain* offers fresh perspectives, challenges dominant narratives, and fosters a more nuanced and complex understanding of Britain and its place in the world. The anthology manifests the hope that through the power of poetry and creative writing, we can cultivate empathy and envision and bring about a more just world - one in which Britain acknowledges its role in the subjugation, exploitation and exclusion of so many, and takes concrete steps towards redress and reparations. By dismantling systems of oppression and exclusion, and committing to anti-racist practices, we can work towards a life-affirming future that upholds the dignity and rights of all people, regardless of race, ethnicity, nationality, or socio-economic status.

Munya Radzi
Regularise
London, April 2023

Sandra A. Agard
Welcome to Britain

The man looked at the piece of paper. This was the right address.

He sighed. He could not take another rejection but he had no choice. Taking a deep breath, he rang the doorbell.

Shuffling steps approached. The door opened to reveal a bespectacled English woman in a pink pinafore. Her eyes blinked when she saw the young Black man dressed in a brown zoot suit, with a grey suitcase on her doorstep.

"Can I help you?" she asked, eyeing him suspiciously.

"Good day, Madame. I was told you had a room for rent."

"Where're you from?" she asked.

"British Guiana."

"You're one of those West Indian boys. Sorry. I ain't got no rooms."

"Madame, I can pay. I have a job," he said hastily.

"You look like a nice young man but my boarders won't take to your kind. You understand?"

She quickly closed the door.

Crumpling the paper, he turned and walked away.

"Welcome to Britain," he said into the cold morning air.

1

Sarfraz Ahmed
Around Here

I remember the bread and butter drama
Of the kitchen sink
When the plates went flying
I began to think

Hiding in my bedroom
I became another teenager
Lost in rock and roll
The music went through my ears
And consumed me whole

Out of my bedroom window I could see
Kids playing with skipping ropes and other things
I would often join them in the park
And ride on the swings

In the summer
I'd sit and watch the girls go by
Although we never got the courage
To go up to them and give it a try .

I'd spend hours lying on the grass
Looking at the shapes the clouds made
Just having fun
Doing this and more
In the hot summer sun

A day lasted forever
But we still wanted more
Even after we'd eaten all the bubble gum
From the playground floor

Now I am all grown up
And a thousand miles away
I sometimes think of those days
I think about these memories

And wish they'd never disappear
The memories of my childhood
When I used to live around here

Jim Aitken
Pastuso in Rwanda

First they came for my dear friend, Mr Samuel Gruber,
who came originally from Hungary, I think
Then they came for me early one Friday morning.
They burst into my attic bedroom as I slept
and shouted, *'Get your filthy foreign fur out of this bed.'*
I was terribly shocked and embarrassed for my hosts.
The children, Judy and Jonathan, were screaming and Mr
and Mrs Brown protested rather profusely, as I recall.

No longer welcome, I was whisked out of 32 Windsor Gardens
without even being able to say all my goodbyes
and without, more importantly, any marmalade sandwiches
for the long journey to Kigali airport. There was to be no
legal appeal on my behalf owing to the fact that my
anthropomorphised identity was not considered to be legal.
I simply could not understand the complexities of it all and
found it rather sad for the country I once considered my home.

My biographer, that nice Mr Michael Bond, had once witnessed
the *Kindertransport* refugees on their arrival in London
with labels round their necks, and so he simply transferred
this to me. It was my lovely Aunt Lucy who had enabled me
to stowaway and she placed a message around my neck
which read, *'Please look after this bear. Thank you.'*
I did have a wonderful time in Notting Hill, looking back,
and I do miss the Brown family and think of them with fondness.

Cleverly, the authorities here in Kigali have requested that
my statue in Paddington Station, along with the other one
in Leicester Square, be sent over here. It certainly seems that
I am marketable everywhere I go. They have built me a nice hut
in the Volcanoes National Park and my new neighbours,
the gorillas, are extremely pleasant and I understand their
language perfectly well. It is similar to the language I spoke
in darkest Peru. In these beautiful mountains I am called Pastuso.

This was my actual name at birth. The Bonds and the Browns, terribly nice people as they were, preferred the name Paddington since foreign sounding names were just too difficult, it seemed. And it also seems, looking back, how it was their so called Brexit that tapped into the fear of the foreign and created the madness engulfing the place. With their economy now belly-flopping, it seems they need a constant stream of diversionary scapegoats. It is all such a terrible shame but it's now time for a jar of marvellous marmalade.

Malka al-Haddad
Roll Without Papers

Since arriving into my British exile, I dreamt of becoming
a famous poet-laureate
I dreamt of writing books of lovers' stories and dozens of books
on the beauty of nature, the likes of which I have not seen,
since I lived forty years in the desert of wars and strife.
I performed my poems to my hungry children and gave them sweets
so that they can praise my poems
I recited my poems to the homeless and the displaced,
to sow hope for them
I was wondering how these poets wrote their poems
Yeats
Plath,
Shakespeare,
Kipling,
Burns,
Oscar Wilde,
Milton
and Keats.
They might go out on a hunting picnic with their dogs
They might go to the bar and flirt with blonde girls while drinking red wine
and listening to the harpsichord
After ten years fighting the Department of Immigration, the dream faded
with the sound of my empty stomach,
faded with the sound of rain eroding the roof of my shelter
faded with frequent knocking on my door
from the immigration housing officer, demanding I leave
It faded with the sound of my broken bike chains,
loaned from the Red Cross
I no longer remember the names of these poets
The titles that I imagined for my books have vanished
And my poems vanished, like these homeless souls
and immigrants without shelter
Last night I was listening to a romantic poet and my British neighbors
shouted, turn off the light, face your dreams with mirage, and
do not follow anyone.

Be yourself in a torn hat, deformed shoes, a false dress and learn how to roll without papers.

Judith Amanthis
apocalypse already

said the uber to the fare
madam
how's your end of empire
to which she replied
staring at the sodium sky
any minute
and he laughed
so sharp
it drove his only asset
full tilt at the city night
whose cruel queen
who he's petitioned end to end
still hasn't died in
fifteen years of endless blindsides
in this locked island
so advancing
its standard of off shore war
it killed his mum and dad
and when he fled it
bricked him in
can't visit his sister
no end in sight but
a work permit for cement
you can only laugh
he said
so mad his end it
fried his eyes
she couldn't see in the dark at her end

Marie Adrien Bitty
When George Floyd Died

A year before George Floyd's death
I crafted a message,
Rolled it,
And put it in a bottle.

I addressed it to the Equal Diverse & Co
And threw it into the sea.

Sh...

I waited on an island,
Watched the sun rise and the stars fall
And the sea each day
As it ebbed and flowed.

When George Floyd died
I saw the air turn blue
And many ships riding the waves
Including the one I sought.

I threw another bottle.
"I am here waiting on this island,
Watching the moon
Wax and wane each night."

After they buried George Floyd,
The wind blew my way.
They sent a company captain.
To rescue or enslave me?

They said I could join them
Use my pain and anger as fuel
To prove my point
And make them all pay.

I asked, "At what price?"
They said, "We cannot pay, only you can."

Sh... Sh... Sh....

I listened to the crashing waves
And bid the company goodbye.
I decided to remain on the island
And create my own paradise.

Anna Blasiak
How To Be An Immigrant

No need to open
Your mouth at all;
When you enter, stay mum.
Smiling is ok. Accent is not.

Don't worry about inviting people to dinner –
Best not to, as that would be foreign.
You could be spotted this way.
Let the dinner go cold.

If mastering tea with milk is too hard,
Choose thirst;
You can never
Dunk properly anyway.

Remember that the black mould in the shower
Comes out to welcome you.
That's what eventually will make you feel
At home.

Inspired by Bertolt Brecht's "On the Term of Exile."

Conor Blessing
Spirit of William Wallace

When King Edward had me cut up like a pig, he got me stuck here as long as Christ. Ceaselessly, ma eyes have been peeled back, watchin ma brothers, ma sisters an oor allies in Wales an Ireland have their tongues ripped oot. But Ah've grown powerful enough in that time tae dae somehing aboot it. Noo free tae walk among the livin again, Ah will finally free us all fae the false gods o this 'Kingdom.' Keep strong, ma friends.

William Wallace (c.1270 – 1305) was a 13th century Scottish revolutionary. After John Balliol abdicated as King of Scots, Edward I invaded Scotland in 1296 to claim rulership with an English command. This resulted in a growing revolution which Wallace had a major role in. He was appointed 'Guardian of Scotland' following the success of the Battle of Stirling Bridge in 1297. He later stepped down from this title in 1298 following the defeat at Falkirk and went into hiding before being arrested in 1305. After being found guilty of treason, Wallace was hung, drawn and quartered. To this day, he is remembered and celebrated as a symbol of Scottish Independence. While his life has been adapted for screen (Braveheart, 1995), that adaptation is largely inaccurate.

Paul Brookes
Refugee

is good. To belong
is wrong. Be homeless.

Mortgages and rents are chains.
Tread the world without burden.

Find a banquet in a crumb.
A glassful in a droplet.

Warmth in a newspaper blanket.
Comfort is a concrete underpass.

Martin Brown
How Do You Do?

I learned your language long ago,
It still feels strange and new;
You're silent when I say *Hello!*
And ask you, *How do you do?*

The weather, it's quite different here,
The trees and houses, too.
The sounds and smells seem so strange,
Tell me, how do you do?

My brother hasn't got here yet,
They wouldn't let him through;
My father disappeared last year,
Tell me, how do you do?

Wherever I walk, people gawp,
I feel I'm in a zoo.
Am I really that unusual?
Tell me, how do you do?

My time, I'm told, is limited,
I'm sorry, I thought you knew,
I'd hoped to stay and hear you say:
Tell me, how do you do?

Helen Buckingham
Haiku

high table
a parliament of crows
breaking bread

Philip Burton
Europium

1.
There is an element of surprise
that, in nineteen oh one, they chose

europium to name a new metal;
not hard for us to see the parallel

with Europe back then – hugely volatile –
needing to cool, congeal.

Had Europe simply Europeanised,
become a single element at that time;

had its fragility been self-observed
and the barrels of guns repurposed

as magnificent city organ pipes;
had it furnished scientific minds

with a vital compass of compassion
so, when chancing on unstable atoms,

instead of breeding cosmic mayhem
researchers would have re-interred them

for fear of unleashing evils to come –
but no, we're saddled with *plutonium.*

2.
Old radioactive atoms turn leaden –
as do spent powers like Britain.
A world of exclusively inert nations
might constitute a more peaceful place

but *plumbum* does a rum thing, alas,
oozing down the stained glass

a full inch every thousand years.
Indeed, all history one day disappears.

The UK, peering past its hospital mask
yearns for a long-unfinished task

to resurrect. And this last firework can,
appearing to be dead, burn our hand.

Richard Byrt
Welcome Back to Britain: The Veteran's Return

1.
Yes. Till 1796, I spent fifty-seven years at sea.
Salt beef and *biscuits*. Thrashed, as a lad, by the bo'sun,
with *the end of a rope*. But soon,
proudly aloft as a *topman*.

Now, at 75, I'm forced to ask
for money on *White Moss* Common.
All I own in two bags. Only a barn for shelter. A lady
gave me a coin and a smile

that touched my heart. I rejoiced
to hear larks rising on Loughrigg Fell, watch sun
set, amber gold, over Grasmere.

2.
Seven years in the Army. 2023, but I'm forced
to ask for money on Gallowtree Gate.
After Iraq, Afghanistan, my mate's
brains shot out in front of me.

Now all I own in two bags.
Only a doorway for shelter. A passer-by
spits. Another one tosses a coin.
All they see is a tramp. They don't know

I've fought for my country, played in a band. They don't see
my determination to carry on seeking
a home, a job, a man to love.
Once again play my guitar.

Make music like you.

Very sadly and appallingly, veterans facing homelessness in Britain is not a new phenomenon. The first part of "Welcome Back to Britain: The Veteran's Return" is based on an extract from Dorothy Wordsworth (1801) *The Grasmere Journals,* from which the name "White Moss" is taken.

Passages in italics in the first stanza are from BBC History (2014), "Life at Sea in the Royal Navy at the End of the Eighteenth Century", available at:
http//:www.bbc.co.uk/history/british/empire_seapower/fill_at_sea_01.html Accessed 21 October 2016.

Gareth Calway
All Together In This

From the council Estates
To the posh ones with Parks,
From high fashion and high finance
To their slave kids in the dark;

From the Poles to the Equator
Supermoon into eclipse,
From the fjords to the deserts
Temperate zones to the tropics…

Can't breathe…

Come and heal us with your caring
Then go back where you came,
You're not from round here
We don't know your name;

From the centre of the cosmos
To Little England in the Styx,
From the heart of Little England
To each human breath's limits…

Can't breathe…

Blitzing Brits for Blighty
As the Beast from the East
Spits his cold War into Salisbury
Then we go off piste;

Playing truant from the Test,
Now we're top of Death's class,
Lord Hee Haw dressed as Churchill
We are such a silly ass.

Can't breathe…

Yuan Changming
My Crow

As an ancient Chinese saying goes
Crows everywhere are equally black
But this one in the heart of England
Is as white as a summer cloud
I have fed him with fog and frost
Until his feathers, his flesh
His calls and even his spirit
All turned into white like winter washed

My crow's wings will never melt
Even when flying close to the sun

Jo Cheadle
Ola and Victoria

The yellow angel balances atop a pale pillar where the stone monarch sits. Barbary lions guard its border as the Union Jack flies above the huge, empty house beyond. Victoria's memorial is vast, proud, costly, its gilded roots running deep, through the Earth, touching every continent.

Below its base, Ola sits with her son in the cosy afternoon light. Her hands enclose his, like a delicate shell around a pearl. Her thoughts are consumed by the mold spreading steadily throughout their one-bed flat. Tourists step around them.

The sunlight shifts. Victoria's wintry shadow grows longer, ushering Ola out of sight.

Marcus Christopherson
Queuing

For hundreds of years
We've sat back as a nation,
Abandoned our post
And deserted our station.

"Red, white and blue?
Little room for black."

"White to the front,
And rest to the back."

You are guilty
As I am too.
For forgetting our conscience
And skipping the queue.

"As long as mine are alright
It's not a problem."

"Place in line, more important,
Don't care who is trodden."

The British traditionally
Love a queue.
But some things you can't wait for.

"Please, after you."

David Clark
Uncle Henry
On his 90th birthday, September 2013

1939 Uncle Henry fled Berlin
All alone to Manchester, aged 15.
He spoke no English, no more school,
but factory work for him.

Teased at work, teased in the hostel,
Henry put on a brave face.
Always smiling, no use complaining,
a kind word for everyone, a joke or two.

Henry played the piano, joined a band,
gigs in pubs, always smiling, a joke or two.
Now 90 years of age, still in Manchester, still alone,
a kind word for everyone, a joke or two.

My uncle, Henry Walton, came to Britain through what came to be known as the Kindertransport in the spring of 1939.

A C Clarke
Unreadable

Officious hi-viz jackets buzz with colour.
Fresh-landed migrants hunch inside sodden clothes,
eyes down. But one is looking ahead.

A house, a normal house, sits on the shore
alongside beach huts. One of the jackets
seems to be pointing it out. The two men,
both of a height, lean towards each other
as friends might do sharing a confidence.

A blue-grey wash colours the landscape
neutral; the sea is flat as an iron.

Julian Colton
The Bird Singing

It seems to me
sings the bird singing in the tree

we're even less free
than we ever used to be

and everywhere there's more inequality
a shortage of integrity

money controlled by oligarchies
wage and outright slavery

disguised by commodities
internet, mobiles and TV

advertising's banality
we're still chained to machinery and technology.

And these questions of identity
black and white, class, gender and sexuality

come between the unity of you and me.
So, I'll sing in this tree

of the differences, similarities
between you and me

sings the bird singing in the tree.

Mark Connors
Cut Here

I learn a lot while you cut my hair,
snipping away without nicking my ears.
How you run in the hills – sixty miles a week,
Take a dip in Keighley Lake when you come off Curlew Hill.
A curry once a fortnight with the lads.

You did alright through lockdowns – it made you think.
No point just sitting here waiting, listening
to folk rant about Brexit Five Live.
You cut by appointment these days.
Can't believe they still bleat on about it.
Boris got it done, and Covid while he was at it.
You did alright with your bar in Malaga.
You can afford to take it easier.
You get a good rent for the flat upstairs.

Barbers haven't half changed, I say.
When I was a lad, it was Gerard or Frank Coakley.
You came out with a short-back-and-sides
no matter what you asked for.
A lolly or a cuppa for your trouble.
Where's my treat? I ask.
There's been too many handouts, you reply.
You laugh but it's not funny.
Then you start on immigration policy.

Mark Connors
Grandma's war on drugs

I remember how easy it was to charm
the vein from your forehead when I questioned
every racist comment you made,
like when you said there were no drugs in Leeds before the war
until the Jamaicans and West Africans came.
Thank fuck they did. They took jobs the dead couldn't fill.
I'd tell you about film stars and singers who used drugs,
how The Beatles wrote their best stuff on weed and LSD
and how The Victorians adored them as much as true crime and sex.
I'd tell you how Sherlock Holmes cherished his opiates
and could never solve a case until he had chased the dragon
and that he played the violin better when he was off his tits.
He's not even real, you'd scream. No, but Arthur Conan Doyle was.

We didn't get on in your later years,
despite your indefatigable love for me
and for always having time and a fiver for my son
and telling me bedtime stories when my mother had none.
But even when you thought you *could* say things like that
you never once questioned whether you should.

Diana Coombes
War Zone

What are those planes, Mummy,
hovering in the sky?
They're making such a sound, Mummy,
making my teddy cry.
Stay away from the window,
take this bag and pack.
Dry those tears, my darling.
Hurry. I'll be right back.
What will I pack, Mummy?
Can I take teddy too?
Of course you can, darling,
but your clothes, only a few.
Where will we go Mummy?
Will we take our car?
No, we'll take a little walk.
It really isn't far.

Cardinal Cox
The Flag of my Britain has More than Three Colours

My Britain has
Roads built by Romans
Laws written by Normans
Fish and Chips fried by Sephardic Jews
NHS filled with global nurses
A flag of more than 3 colours

My Britain has
A language Anglo-Saxon
A church formed by Germans
Take-away staffed by Vietnamese
A lawyer, who represents me, from Uganda
A flag of more than 3 colours

My Britain has
Cities built by Vikings
Silk woven by Huguenots
Footballers from Spain, South America, Eastern Europe...
A Somali refugee at the Olympics
A flag of more than 3 colours

My Britain has
Millionaires and beggars, politicians and priests,
Police officers and criminals, military and peace campaigners,
Grafters and shirkers, union members and entrepreneurs,
Students and professors, patients and doctors,
A flag of more than 3 colours

Heaven Crawley
Whiteness

The privilege of whiteness
Is never having to think about
The colour of my skin

Never having to walk down the street
With my sleeves pulled down over my hands
To stop the names
The stares
The spit
Of those that pass

The privilege of whiteness
Is never having to worry
That my son will be stopped
For no reason
Keep his mouth shut
But not too shut
Comply
Or potentially die

The privilege of whiteness
Is never having to wonder
Whether the job I wanted
Never came
Because of my name
My history
Because of who I am
The discomfort of others
The awkward glances
The 'race card'

The privilege of whiteness
Is the right to be offended
Upset
Angry
If that privilege is questioned

Or even mentioned

The right to be offended that the hurt and pain of others
The insults
The racism
The violence
Could be more important than the gravestone of a dog called 'Nigger'

The privilege of whiteness
Is knowing that I can walk through a border
More easily than a woman from the country next door
Wave my passport
Show my face
Smile
And it's enough
Because the privilege of whiteness will protect me
Keep me safe

The privilege of whiteness
Is the refusal to see it
Acknowledge it
Hear it
See it
Check it
To deny the reality of others
Even when that reality means
Blood
And sweat
And tears

To dismiss those who fight the injustices
As snowflakes
Fake news
Political correctness gone mad

The privilege of whiteness
Follows me
Wherever I go
A blanket of security

Self knowing
Self worth

The privilege of whiteness
Is never having to think about
The colour of my skin

'Nigger' was the name given to a black Labrador dog who was the mascot of the famed 617 Squadron (Dambusters) at RAF Scampton. In 2020, the RAF replaced the dig's gravestone with one that didn't include the dog's name because of the offence caused by the use of the N-word. There was a public petition to get the headstone reinstated on the basis that its removal was an example of 'political correctness gone mad'. See https://thelincolnite.co.uk/2020/07/over-21k-want-racial-slur-dogs-name-back-on-gravestone/

Robin Daglish
Cruel Britannia

It's time to atone:
the statues are tumbling,
slavery, once celebrated
and set in stone is coming
off its pedestals.
We've changed the script,
torn up the rules.
Now even Colston is head first
into the harbour
where his slave ships anchored.

Racism, an ancient word,
starts with perverted histories.
I was brought up in the nineteen fifties
to be proud of the red on the World map:
"all that, belongs to us,"
as if we had been invited round for a cup
of tea,
as if people should be grateful and subservient
for the privilege of being colonised,
and didn't they all love our queen?

The truth is more obscene,
only as an adult did I open my eyes,
realise what a horror story
the grab for empire was.
This is where racism was conceived,
when even the poorest slum dweller
thought himself superior
to an African slave.
And as the Nazis showed us,
when you reduce humans to animal status,
it excuses all sorts of cruelty:
the trafficking of slaves across the sea.

Black lives have always mattered.

Emer Davis
Binned

Glasgow
its green agenda
in tatters

stages dismantled

placards
dumped in jumbo bins

recycled posters
demanding climate change
clogging up the drains

this is the future
mobile and aloof

it's all over now
as they board
the train home

hope forgotten
in the recycled tote bag
they left behind.

Craig Dobson
The Britannia Line, 2016
with Hal, Liz and Winston

Sleek through the rain, its lights aimed at the future,
our half-full train glides up the same route
with which Orwell closed *Homage to Catalonia.*
A bombless drizzle sifts our view. Ponds sulk and rivers brown,
lone farmhouses and huddled villages are pasted with the grey day's shine.

At each stop, London's calling.
When the music starts, heads bob like birds to confirm
its jazz style film score is not a ringtone or forgotten alarm.
It's a while before its riffs calm our ruffled feathers,
realigning them with the myth of a lost theme's long ago.

The marrow notes bleed black and white. Low clouds' tumbled gouts
are slung behind us as the windows mist, cigarette smoke-thick.
Beyond them, tile hung weatherboarded cottages retreat into medieval fields
of timeless sheep, or bow-stringed hop bines drawn towards the sky.
At a crossing, girls in floral dresses on bicycles with baskets wave as we go by.
But the woods blacken with a growing soot of shadow.

Past towns of bay-windowed houses, we gather towards our capital.
Borne on the rails' hypnotic notes and the music's back and forth flow,
we make through sombre streets where hatted couples hurry
past doors sandbagged against the coming downpour, making for
the underground, scanning the heavens through masks of worry.
Coming into sight, Parliament and St Pauls brave lowering skies.
Beside them the grim Thames grinds on.

The brakes scream and the music finally dies as we prepare to alight.
Conditions gentled, we band together, march down the platform
to commit ourselves to the barriers and the multitudes beyond,
our advantage having shown that we can ride out whatever
the cost as long as we never surrender this new journey's
old resolve to go on to the end, even in the dust;
if necessary for years, if necessary alone.

The last verse contains mangled fragments of quote from Shakespeare's *Henry V*, Elizabeth I's 1588
Tilbury speech and Churchill's 1940 'We shall fight on the beaches' speech.

Kimia Etemadi
Engelestân

You would too, though. Wouldn't you? You would move, too.
You would take your six-month-old baby across continents too, if it meant
she would be allowed to ride a bicycle despite being a girl...
only to be told by an elderly white woman:
"I don't know what they do in *your country*, but here,
you're NOT ALLOWED to ride on the pavement!"
Just seven years old, she was more confused than upset.
"Mummy, what did that lady mean? What's *my country*?"
And how should you respond when your daughter tells you
a friend in nursery asked why her skin is *that* colour?
"Mummy, why *is* my skin different?"
But anything would surely be better than the flogging, the torture,
the executions, the mass graves...
After five years of imprisonment for being a Marxist, such depression
could only have been cured by leaving Iran.
Welcome to Britain.
You have to start from zero here. Thirty-eight years old? It doesn't matter.
Zero means *zero*.
Your beautiful hand-woven rugs are later brought to you.
They depict mythical birds, Persian legends, and paradise.
"So exotic," your new compatriots say.
But you don't want to ask your English friends to take their shoes off.
The rugs, hundreds of years old, passed from ancestor to descendant—
all that you have left of your culture—and yet:
"Come in. Keep your boots on. It's fine."
Drink your tea and just try your best to not think about it.

"Engelestân" means "England" in Persian, my mother tongue.

James Farson
Bretton Library, Rightwell East

The battleship of a circ desk is gone

The train and bus in the kids area remain

And still it has a better collection of graphic novels than it
Has any right to.

No longer in the centre of the community
But it is the centre

With its knit and natter
Rhymetime
Storytime
Computer courses
Strategy game club
Rentable rooms
Study space coming soon
Plenty of computers
Free Wi-Fi
Knowledgeable friendly staff

And air conditioning.

Do you know how many libraries in Peterborough have air conditioning?

It is the centre

And it has held
And it holds

A door open,
For you,
Whoever you are
Whatever you need

Come to the feast.

Max Terry Fishel
My mother Renate arrives in England in 1947

She came with a dictionary, but war needs
no translation, she already had the vocabulary
of persecution -

"Are you Jewish? You don't look Jewish" She
wonders what Jewish looks like but there is
too much weight on her shoulders to shrug
and give the stereotype an outing -

Will they kill me here, she wonders as she
joins a queue for processing in the new
country; she glances round, is relieved to
see there are no showers here

although she needs one.

Uncircumcised men press necessary new
papers on her, ration book, identity card,
train ticket, she can smell the steam as she
reads her destination, her destiny but she is
unnerved by the engine *it has an oven belching
smoke* and there is smut on her face, tiny
traces of someone's history and her heart
lurches for her own (*how could anyone do this?*)

In Liverpool she meets handsome Maurice;
his story is no easier than hers, which makes
hers easier to bear; together when she has
learned the English words of love, they will
make me, but not in their own image, their
DNAs entwining like their bodies in their liberated
lovemaking, a position not known in the Talmud,
and I am born, innocent at first, until I learn.

Max Terry Fishel
Guns at Euston

I saw it, said it, but it wasn't
sorted and now there are guns
at Euston, protecting the timetable
of our little days with a thin finger.

(The escalators don't care,
they take you as you are,
bomb or no bomb, love
or none, dogs must be carried.
I have no dog to carry.)

On the sly concourse
a camera turns its poor eye to me
almost like a friend with a question
almost like a mother with a jemmy
to prise me open on the platform
to see if I too have a timer, to see
how long I have left -

Max Terry Fishel
England is a hard place

Bliss in the town, till the next high
rise. There are drugs here, down
alleys, in bankers' creamy toilets;
your job is to ambulance the ODs;
your job is to bless them, father,
for England is a hard place.

In DNA kiosks in the night, under
bleary bulbs on the road to the bridge,
lovers share needles and hindsight
over a map of the forsaken world; we
are nearly America now as the bricks
rot; cry, for England is a hard place.

The child is ill-clothed, ill-fed, and
ill. The child is English, and can prove
it in a test, but the canvas flag is too
heavy and she falls and becomes
foreign. No-one can spell *foreign*, but
it is the worst thing to be, for England
is a hard place.

Corinne Fowler
Kings Heath Park
Birmingham, England

I pass them on my first lap:
three walkers in tracksuits and duffles.
India, Kashmir and Pakistan in suburban step.

On lap two,
they forage for mulberries,
probing branches with a walking stick.

On the third lap
the trio meet my eye,
welcome a companion to their ritual.

Running, I remember all the times
I've eavesdropped on their talk
of cancer and cricket,
a busman's strike,
visas denied,
footwear,
diabetes,
a faraway grave.

They smile at me on my last lap.
Sunset makes toggles gleam,
lights eye-wicks, smears cheeks with gold.

By the Spring they've outstripped Gandhi,
not with salt marches but ambles along grass-fringed paths
where something new begins with crocus and celandine.

Corinne Fowler
Cotswolds
Snowshill Village

The map confounds us.
We feed horses, follow walls, cross hobbled fields.

We peep over limestone:
buds smoke, bees drone.

Hamida climbs a wall.
Her veil's a flag I follow,
ignoring nettles, boundaries, Lana's pleas.

We enter a lavender field,
roam combed rows.

Hamida twists a stem
and hands Lana a sprig:
"*lavender arabica*" she says.

"Loot", I say.
We grin and get to work,
hugging armfuls, tugging roots.

"Reminds me of Provence!" I call.
"Matches my bathroom!" Hamida retorts.
We stop.

A tractor putters across the hill.

Voices: we are rabbits
fearing farmers, dogs, diesel, wire.

Words drift, cornstalks crunch, ramblers pass by.

"Got the lavender?" I ask.
"Loot", says Lana, brandishing her bunch.

Mirth grips us: the field weeps blue, indigo, violet.

Back on the footpath we steal a last look.
The lavender stands stiff-stalked, club-headed.

Corinne Fowler
Myrtilla
St. Lawrence Church Oxhill, 1705

Six men shoulder your pall,
servants with your complexion.
The coffin scrapes a buttress:
your knuckle raps the casket base.

Beauchamp's arm shoots up.
The procession halts.

Mr. Beauchamp's called a gentleman,
you, his cargo,
shipped from Nevis Island
to Queen's Square.

You saw everything. Said nothing.
Gave away the tenderness you craved,
raised the masters Beauchamp,
nursed and cradled waifs of a life unlived.

Myrtilla, evergreen
with showers of gold.

Your tomb cold-shoulders the family plot
        Myrtilla
        Black Girl
        Negro Slave
Lichens grow. Earth breathes. Grasses weave.

Paul Francis
Home Office Briefing

Maintain the narrative:
tradition of safe haven, refugees.
*The Kindertransport…*you know how it goes.

Ukraine was an emergency.
Europe scrapped visas, let them all come in.
We kept the visas. We took back control.
Say there's a family of five.
Issue four visas, keep the fifth one back.
What family would leave one kid behind?
Result. Four visas out, no bodies in.

Come the Press Conference, this is how it goes.
Don't answer any questions, just
maintain the narrative:
tradition of safe haven, refugees.
The Kindertransport. Visas handed out…

Paul Francis
Drawing the Line

What is so special about Ukrainians?

A time of crisis – urgent human need.
So let them come, provide support;
free access, jobs, and stay in people's homes.

The Afghans think: so they get homes?
Eleven thousand of us stuck
in crap hotels – and they get homes?

The Syrians think: our house blown up
by Russian troops, led by the general
who blew up theirs - and they get jobs?

North Africans who're stuck in Calais think
we've been here months
– and they get flown straight in?

We're not so special, say Ukrainians.
The West is cautious, calculates.
They need stuff in reserve;
this is rehearsal, not the main event.

They're scared we'll lose
and terrified we'll win.
Get Putin mad and that might mean
they end up with a proper war
where Westerners would die.

Marsha Glenn
A Piece of Stolen Time

I am standing in the middle of the South Asian craft collection, brought by the British Empire to the heart of London. These items made a long journey from the Indian subcontinent to today's Great Britain, where millions can see but none can touch or feel them.

I can also see the soldiers of Her Majesty's government come to the famous craftsman's house to order unique embroidery for the royal family. Everyone from the neighbourhood is gathered outside the craftsman's house. He is shaking, standing with his palms pressed together as if he has done something terrible and is asking for mercy.

I wonder, did he get fair remuneration for his craftsmanship? How much? And how much did Zamindar, the appointed landlord, demand in tax on those earnings?

Barrington Gordon
Black & White TV Sound Bites: A Colourful War

IMAGE: Skeletal buildings with innards torn out, hanging wires. Twisted
　　concrete.

"WARNING: Distressing images of War." BBC Strap Line.
THOUGHT: But war is distress. Needs no warning. We need
　　to be distressed.
"Until the colour of a man's skin is of no more significance
　　than the colour of his eyes – War!" Bob Marley.

IMAGE: Soldier carries child in yellow coat; contrasted with
　　combat fatigues.
THOUGHT: *Dulce et decorum est.*
"It is sweet and fitting to die for one's country."
Who asked Africans if they wanted to be sacrificial lambs?

The clarion call of the futility of war is unheeded. As bodies, over the
centuries, are stacked high.
The stench reaches heavenly skies.
The nostrils of God are closed.
Tears fall. The blood of innocents flows.

IMAGE: Missiles
THOUGHT: Missiles of hatred rent the skies, hungry for human flesh.

"This is not our war. We need to leave this place."
THOUGHT: But all routes to escape have been cut off.
Footages explode in my mind. Man-kind?

"No supplies coming in, nothing going out…"
THOUGHT: Tanks, heavy artillery can be bought off shelves.
Weapons of mass destruction supplied and bought by fat bellies
but no bread in shops to eat. Iron roams freely where humans once trod.
"We are students, not fighters."
"We want to go."
"Only Ukrainians…"

IMAGE: Ample buses to transport people to safety.
THOUGHT: We can't be seen as human then.
"Many are treated as second class citizens…"

IMAGE: Crowds of calm Black people waiting behind barbed wire fences.
THOUGHT: Inside I'm screaming. I know they must be too.

"They are not allowing any Black people to enter inside the gates…"

IMAGE: Young African men.
THOUGHT: I can see death in their eyes as they fight for hope.

"If you are Black you must walk."
"It was horrible…"
"It was uncalled for…"
"It was deeply inhumane."

IMAGE: Snow covered Black people. A young mother struggles
    to bottle feed baby in freezing snow.
THOUGHT: Her plaited cornrows of black hair furrowed with snow.
Numb normality.
"Caught up in conflict…"

IMAGE: Civilized streets.
"We don't have light…"
"We don't have water…"
"And now the battery will be low…"
THOUGHT: Black clouds explode from the earth, kiss the sky.
Routes cut off.
Future,
African.

"We are scared…"
THOUGHT: I am scared just watching… for you… for us.
"We are really scared…"
"Please help us…"
"I don't even know which English word to use…"

A picture of a young African woman in front of a lustrous

50

colourful Christmas tree
smiles back at me.
"Terrified…"

THOUGHT: Black children born in Ukraine now know
    they are not white.

IMAGE: Normality. Brown skinned children playing tag.
Colourful elastic band braided plaits.
THOUGHT: A colourful war.

IMAGE: Train stations packed but no passage to get out.
"Filming in the very same train stations they are trying to flee from…"
THOUGHT: Water so desperately needed by humans flows across
    bombed bridges scattered like pieces of a puzzle as human ants chart
    a trail across to escape.

"Ukrainian men between the ages of 18 and 60 are forbidden to leave
    the country…"
THOUGHT: So why are you not letting non-Ukrainians go?
I am not your enemy.

"Families are split as women and children are trying to get to safety…"
THOUGHT: Trains only laid on for Ukrainians… Why?

IMAGE: A white hand presses against a train window. A white child
    looks out smiling from the other side.
"They are not allowing any Black people…"

IMAGE: Dark of Black people trapped. Trying to flee
THOUGHT: I want to turn off this Black & White TV.

At the press of a button, could I end this war?

Roger Griffith
Of Riots & Rebellions

Just when does a riot signify a rebellion?
Well, let me remind you when communities took to the streets
To defend their dominion.

The difference, for some, can be a matter of colour,
But, for many others, it's a matter of honour.

I remember when, as a boy-man just about to leave school,
The frontline of St Pauls was no places for fools.

How can you possibly understand
When a person has reached the end of their tether?
Fed up with ritual police humiliation and the sound of skinheads' leather.

For when Black lives and blue lines mash,
It becomes more than just a culture clash.

And so it began on April 2nd, 1980,
When the Black & White cafe exploded into flames,
Its raging occupants lighting up media headlines forever
With infamous fame.

The indigo skies were lit from the blaze
And the sirens blared for miles around,
Whilst down below,
Broken glass, desperate cries and shouts
Provided the street-sounds.

In those moments there was no reasoning, no reckoning,
No time for sorrow,
Just 'Get Up Stand Up' with little hope offered for brighter tomorrows.

Toxteth, Brixton, Handsworth and Broadwater Farm came next,
From a people pushed beyond being merely vexed.

Some say, "A crime is a crime,
So those responsible must be punished and silenced!"
Ignoring state complicity in SUS laws, mass unemployment and violence.

After the school gates closed, I learned resistance
And uprisings were commonplace
In order to preserve Black lives with grace.

Nanny of the Maroons, Bussa, Quamina and Sam Sharpe
Led Caribbean rebellions
Against the evils of the slave trade,
A trade that made many in Bristol and Britain millions.

Mandela and Martin Luther King Jr went to prison,
Resisting with actions that were complementary
To the Black Panthers and Bernie Grant's "By Any Means Necessary."

Today Black Lives Matter and fresh activists take forward these mantras.
Others, like me, tackle social injustice with stanzas.

So, I can understand,
Depending on your point of view,
That this tale will make you feel black or blue.

But whether you call it a riot or a rebellion matters not the least,
As we return to the days when people go cold and hungry,
While the elite feast.

Rosario Guimba-Stewart
The Paper

She got it!
It was the widest smile I'd ever seen.
Her perfectly formed white teeth
Couldn't hide her happiness.
She gave me the tightest hug.
I could hardly breathe.
And in her nearly teary-eyed voice,
She told me she'd got it.

She'd waited years
And many times, she'd lost hope.
In her darkest moments, she'd contemplated ending it all.
The sufferings. The uncertainty. Her life.

But she'd hung on.
The people around her gave her strength.
Chatting, laughing, grabbing all opportunities
In the hope that one day the training would be of use,
The networking would bear fruit
And her rights would be restored.

She said she got it!
She got it!
She got it!
I can get a job!
I can study!
I can stay and build my life with my daughter,
The reason for it all. The love that kept me going.

She said she got it!
She couldn't contain her joy.
She said thank you so many times
I lost count!

She'd got it!
Now life has to move on.

New beginnings.
New challenges.
And she couldn't wait!

Prabhu S. Guptara
Survival

I speed along these rolling hills,
These leafy vales, till I'm slowed down
In village where there's thatch on roofs,
And landscaped gardens overflow.

Admiring here the makes of cars
Along the streets, the garages
Of generous size, I chance upon
A pub – a pub! Just what I need!

The food is good, astonishing
An English village this remote.
As is the sunshine lighting up
Each glass, each chink - encouraging

A treacherous thought: why not a walk?!
And so I ask the publican,
How far the village centre is.
He hums, and haws, and "Well", he says

"Straight down the road it is, though you
Might miss our little village hall.
There is a bit of green… we used
To have a football team, we still

Have cricket… and there's then the church,
Eternal, solid, by the store,
Which doubles as our post office,
And just about survives - like us".

Monique Guz
Helpline

Where... do I even start?

Closed windows. Drawn curtains.
A heatwave. In a pandemic. In a recession.
Cancelled flights. Rail strikes.
Fire. Sewage. Drought.
Farm fields without crops.
Nature reserves without wildlife.
Factory workers without unions.
The sick, the poor, the stateless.
The cold, the hungry, and homeless.
Austerity, deregulation, privatisation.
Retrain and find other jobs!
Key workers on picket lines. Wars and raids.
Stay alert! Hide in a fridge! Now is not the time.
Tax havens. Deportations. Two-tier systems.
Lefty-lawyers. Do-gooders. Public nuisance!
The never-ending fatigue of never-ending crises.
Get Brexit done! Clap for PPE contracts!
The cost of living in a gig economy.
The flat you can't move out of. The house you can't move into.
The cost of loving in a hostile environment.
The parents who need you. The children you want.
50% funding cuts. Scrap the arts. English literature. And media literacy.
Scrap music. Comedy. And critical thinking.
Omitted histories in the classroom. Don't protest!
Glass ceilings in the workplace. Don't organise!
Mansplaining white saviours. Victim-blaming tech bosses.
Microaggressions and macroeconomics. Greenwashing. Gatekeeping.
Empty shops. Food banks. And spin the wheel!
Mouldy bread. Tin foil. And kettles.
More parties, wallpaper, and luxury flats!
Your entire community - for let (up 15%)!
The death rattle of a collapsing system.
Strong and stable. Special measures.
Waiting lists shortened with every suicide.

Student loan debt. Energy bill debt.
Biological clock. Doomsday clock.

But I cannot verbalise any of it.
And no anxiety or depression webinar can address
What it is to be woke.

Kim Hackleman
If Godiva Awoke Today

If Godiva awoke today
Would she have to petition
Her husband to listen
By riding through the streets
Of Coventry bareback
With no clothes on
While Peeping Tom
Watches drooling
Out of his window?

Or would it be her
Leading the way
To make certain
That those in the city
Who suffer grievously
(For whatever reason)
Cease their suffering
That the wealth be distributed evenly
That the opportunities be offered to all
That no child go hungry
No human be killed
And the most vulnerable among us
Find strength through their community?

In her moment of decision
Would she be as hesitant
As Leighton depicts?

Or would she
Marvel with impatience
At the lack of action and empathy and understanding
Of those elected or paid to serve:
Oaths taken,
Speeches made,
Photos posted,
Tweets tweeted,

And the sweet heads of babies kissed...
And still inequity reigning?

If Godiva awoke today
Would she listen
And would she lead?

scott manley hadley
from 'goth'

There used to be a Woolworths in town, like, but that's gone. Never swish enough for an M&S, there used to be a BHS, there's a Cix, a Boots, Sports Direct... There are shops, yeah, but they're all shops you've seen before and there aren't very many. She wishes there was an All Saints. Or even a Topshop (Topshop sometimes do black). She is the only Goth in town. Her brother's 11 months older than she is. Was that deliberate? Her parents don't talk much. To her, or each other. Dad drinks. Mum drinks. They do not drink together.

Nusrat M Haider
Children of Empire

My grandparents
Came to England
Aboard the Windrush
In their best hats and coats

They toiled
Built the streets
And the NHS
With their spit, sweat and tears

My past, present and future

Brick by brick

They scaffolded the train tracks
Proud contribution

Yet have not forgotten
No Irish no dogs no blacks

A distorted nostalgia

Proud children of empire

Yet I am still not free
Nor do I soar the sky higher

My grandfather
Once a train porter
With buttons that shone
Advises me to follow my dreams

Yet on the streets of London today
With strip and search
Why do I feel undermined?

When in court
Why am I severely punished

Just for being?

M-L Chika Haijima
To My Son

To my son, I write this for you.
For the days when being - just being, gets too hard.
For the days you want answers and get none.
For the days where giving up is easier.
For the days when forgiving is out of reach.

To my son, I write this for you.
Because they will judge.
Because they will be kind - and unkind.
Because they will admire - and be afraid.
Because they will tell you who to be.
Because it's easier for them.

To my son, I write this for you.
To apologise when they ask why you are darker.
To apologise when they ask why you are lighter.
To apologise when they touch your curls without asking.
To apologise when they ask why you speak their language.
To apologise when they ask why you don't.
To apologise if I didn't fight enough.
If I didn't protect you enough.
If I didn't understand enough.

To my son, I write this to you.
To remind you that you were born and raised here, on British soil.
And yet.
Through your veins runs the warmth of the River Tiber
And your heart beats with the banging of the Taiko drums.
Your body moves with the rhythm of reggae,
Whilst your feet stamp hard with the chant of the Maori Haka.

All of this is you my son.

Some days, you will feel this inside you.
Some days, you will feel none - and want none.
Some days, you will belong.

Some days, you won't.

To my son, I write this for you.
To remember that this does not define you.
To remember that this is a privilege.
To remember who you are when you feel lost.
To remember it matters and doesn't matter.
To remember you are beautiful.
To remember to be YOU.

Patricia Headlam
Selective Compensation

When you think about British history
spare a thought for those who were once enslaved.

Abducted from Africa and trapped in a brutal system
toiling and terrorising the life out of their souls.

Did they not deserve to receive compensation
for building enormous wealth for the British Empire?

It's a little-known fact that the British Government
went into debt to end enslavement in its colonies.

In the 19th century, millions paid in compensation
to enslavers for the loss of human 'property'.

Amounting to billions in modern currency.

In the 19th century, no payments made to the enslaved
to compensate for over two centuries of forced labour.

They were trapped in another form of enslavement.
Still toiling. Still terrorised. Still not truly emancipated.

In the 21st century, descendants of the enslaved
unknowingly paid taxes towards clearing the debt.

In the 21st century, British institutions and families
still profit from the compensation paid.

The British Government should pay reparations
to descendants of the enslaved.

Do they not deserve to receive the compensation
their ancestors were denied?

Patricia Headlam
Cure

The colour of madness
padded in white supremacy
should be committed into a cell
to put a permanent stop
to its long spell of murdering,
maiming and defaming a people
it once enslaved.
Four hundred years and counting
of hell beginning with those it stole
from Africa to sell and suffer
to build its empire.
Condemnation cast
onto the blackness of skin.
No buffer to hide behind.
The outward stigma burning
deep internally.
No surprise that lingering lies
leave trauma in minds
from generation to generation.
Negative impact
on the sense of wellness.
A white-made madness.
Force-fed to embed
an eternal feeling of inferiority.
There is a cure though.
Found in the form of a
verbal vaccine for anti-blackness.
Administered into the mind
as an antidote for a system
that still holds up whiteness
as eternally supreme.

Patricia Headlam
Drop Poems

Bombs cause mass destruction.
Whole cities require reconstruction.
But you cannot reconstruct dead bodies.
And how do you repair broken souls.

Bombs are dropped when talks fail.
But it's the people, not politicians
who are the ultimate sacrifice.
It's the people who pay with their lives.

Poems are a peaceful way
to launch an anti-war outcry.
To expose politicians who defend
their lust for war with lies.

Poems inspire life
they should be widely read.
Instead of dropping bombs
drop poems to promote peace.

Alanah Hill
An Account of Black Agency in the Satterthwaite Letterbooks

In Kingston, Jamaica on the 3rd of August 1777,
Benjamin Satterthwaite communicates
the recent Jamaican Slave Insurrection,
a response to the inhumane, mass forced migration of human beings,
adults and children, across the Atlantic Ocean's treacherous passage.

The subsequent rebellions emerged in different forms,
in plantations, on ships, all to fight against societal norms
that saw some as inferior because of the colour of their skin,
and could be exploited, brutalised and forced to work for no payment.
Enslaved people fought back, forcing an embargo,
in which Black resistance, agency and power were overlooked
in the letterbooks.

The power to delay the exporting of goods on ships,
the 'Molly' and 'Dolphin',
was a testament to the strength and autonomy of enslaved people
in the face of abhorrent discipline.
Benjamin Satterthwaite saw the 1776 insurrection
as economically inconvenient and not for what it was:
part of a wider transatlantic freedom movement led by enslaved people.

Louisa Humphreys
Walk in The Park

In the car on the way back from a nightwatch at Greenham
Everyone was super friendly
As they drove me home.
They were extra attentive.
They asked me if I needed help
And accompanied me to my door.

I wondered what this was all about.
Did they think I couldn't get to my own front door
Without supervision?

A few days later I went for a walk in the park
With my boyfriend
Who asked, *Did I know I was epileptic?*

I asked, *Is this some sort of sick joke?*
Of course, I didn't know because I am not...

He went through the events of the car journey from Greenham
From the perspective of the other occupants of the car.
I had lapsed into what I had thought was sleep.
I was tired after a night awake at Greenham.
I went to sleep.
That's what happened.

No, he said.
You had a fit.
You need an appointment with your doctor.
Tell them about your brain problem.

I duly went to the doctor and from there
To a place of electrodes which read my mind
And filed me under "Epileptic."

For years, I was scared to have a bath alone in case I had a fit
    and drowned.

I could not learn to drive, as I was a danger on the road,
To myself and others.

And then there was the issue
Of introducing this new diagnosis to my family.
They refused to accept I had epilepsy.
There was a level of shame in the family,
That one of theirs was defective.
So they chose to believe instead
That their daughter was imagining things.

Cathryn Iliffe
I Don't Hate Russians

No I don't hate Russians
the Donbas mothers who want their sons back
not just a head in a box from the local gangster
the sons who want to be home
the sons who put their guns down and went home

No I don't hate the sons captured, tortured and left to die in the road
        shot in the genitals
the son who died in agony with a spike pushed though the eye
the sons of all the stories that are hidden, censored,
        filtered from our sensibilities

No I don't hate Russians, and, they do love their children too

So many flags to wave - a union jack and a yellow and blue
I might wave a Yorkshire flag if I have to wave anything

And I will always salute the battle tattered Red Army flag of victory
        over fascism
That was raised on the Reichstag in Berlin in 1945
        over Hitler's defeated city
A history that is being rewritten, deleted and denied
The flag of victory, that is illegal in Ukraine,
is now raised on the hills above the city of Kremenets.
It flies by the ancient statues of Scythian warriors
to remember 20 thousand Jews tortured and murdered in that city
by Ukrainians, Poles and Germans
To remember 27 million dead Russians
and another 6 million starved in 1991 by Clinton's Cold War

No I don't hate Russians
I don't hate Poles and Germans
And I don't hate Ukrainians,
The sons who left 8 years ago rather than kill their brothers
the 14 thousand people in Donbas killed before the 'war broke out',
before America or Britain stopped the gas pipeline

The sons who left 10 years ago to get away from the corruption
the poverty, the highest death rate in Europe
and the lies that fly faster than guided missiles

Nnamdi Christopher Iroaganachi
Hello Britain, Goodbye World

I'm on a plane towards the Kingdom. My very first visit.
Foreign Ministry in Abuja is clogged with emails from Downing Street
Like a dirty sink filled with dishes, the remains of an Anglian feast,
Now causing a diplomatic digestive challenge with placards and bandanas
    blowing in the breeze.

Number Ten insists, Mister President, Number Ten insists
    on the union of Nigeria
A smug togetherness similar to ice and mackerels in a Tesco fridge
No part must secede, unity is paramount Parliament insists.
And the Prime Minister has made her views clear; no partition is permitted
And this is Britain's prerogative.

Abuja is in a fit as demonstrations boil out in its boulevards
The police have been sent out to make a red stew of limbs and ligaments
Bullets break whatever is left of your resolve and psychomotor skills. After
    the batons have cracked your cranium, that is.
You can't stoop to poop? Oh, your loss, your predicament.
This is the will of the sovereign, the will of the winner and of the kingdom
    too.

We taxi onto the Heathrow tarmac, my pulse is more stable than ever
I dream of bountiful scoops of Bluecoo ice cream after an English dinner.
Some Scotch whiskey before bedtime with the spectacle of democratic
    squabbling on BBC Parliament.
I hail a black cab. Eighty pounds but no worries, mate.
This is my welcome to the capitalist's dream in the capital of the
    kingdom.

Black cab, white fellow, red love when I compliment the ways of his
    English people
He turns chimney-red and parks by the kerb to issue a firm denial
I must learn my anthropology if he is to convey me to my destination
    peaceably.
Scotsmen are no English he warns. I swallow and nod.
Number Ten has done a number on the Scots too, I see. What about

the Irish and Welsh, I ponder.

I feel as if the world has melted away as the wheels of my cab spin
The alien cultures are behind me. Behind me but somehow baked into a
    dough
A dough of unfeeling uniformity. Part of a senseless supper made of
    semantic soup.
A soup of alphabets, a meal of mourning. Fledgling federal republics and
    somewhat disunited nations and kingdoms.

Well, what is all that to me? England, Scotland, Ireland: the land welcomes
    me.
A welcome as warm as tea which I stir into a phrase: hello Britain, goodbye
    world.

Jade Jackson
Running From A Country

I left my country without packing a bag
As packing would have cost me my life
I have a new country now, which I love very much
And new friends too
But I still miss my family and former friends
Who were ruthlessly murdered.

I had to leave otherwise I would be dead now
I miss some food which I cannot get here
But safety first
I walk with pride and without fear
That someone is behind me
Someone is not going to shoot me from behind.

Only loneliness is a killer
You are confined in a space
With your deepest thoughts
You feel overwhelmed and suffocated
In this little space.

Everything feels empty, internally and externally
You feel as though you are in a never-ending circle
A void in which you feel trapped and lost
Simultaneously unable to breath
Since you are alone
With a numbness inside you
Which cannot stop you from feeling
Suicidal, useless
Not because your new country does not love you
But because you are alone and helpless

athina k
Disciplined

I left Greece in a hurry.
A teenager.
I didn't notice England really
Until many years after I lived in it.
The slow and steady.
The repression of emotion.
The tea served in crisis mode.
England taught me discipline.
Emotional regulation.
Showing up on time.
I thought the English not elegant,
Don't cook well, don't share their feelings.
But.
It is in their hiding
They tell you.
Everything.
Of the fear
Of loss
Of grandeur and power.
Collective identity.
Position in the world.
National destiny.

England showed me countryside
That I previously loathed and ridiculed.
I got my education here.
Eventually a job.
I felt welcomed.
My directness and loud voice
Refreshing, even.
I was happy in England.
With my privileged education and job.
I felt I could live here forever.
I married. An Englishman.
And then.
2015

Brexit
Sooner than later.
That welcome unwelcome
Examination of relationships.
Divorce.

Years of disappointment,
Entrapment
And rebellion.
Crying every night
To reconcile myself
To my choices.
To my friends.
To my enemies.
To my England.
The angst to leave it.

Countless times I left it,
Until the pandemic came
And I had to stay put.
In lockdown.
And then I looked.
I understood
I was never in England.
No.
I was running away from it for years
While living in it.
The depressing government.
The unadmitted racism.
The delusional hiding from self
An art form.
The national pastime.
And the beauty of the meadows
Near my house
I had never walked before.
The people I spoke to
I never knew.
I loved England again
During the pandemic.

The more lockedown, the more I loved England.
And the more I loved to hate England.

My home is here in Brexitland.
I feel welcome and unwelcome.
Disciplined.
Repressed.
Emotionally regulated.
Struggling to indefinitely remain
Without revealing myself.

Ziba Karbassi
London

The man
Who has the whole world under his pointer finger
Is my friend
He is the warden of truth
He is a lover of a flower
Whose petals are dual-colored
And soft-spirited
But sturdy in physicality
Who prefers even light
And has a strange love towards cool shadows

Behind that day
Before that yesterday
Beside that side

The newly-sprouted branch
Around my arm
Awakening my angels
From their slumber
Time after time

Behind that day
Before that yesterday
Beside that side

The city
Whose heart is two opposite swans
Whose love burns like a phoenix
Flies ahead of all
The major cities
In the world

Translated from Persian by Nazlee Radboy

80

John F Keane
How Different This

Toiling homeward along
some street I spied two
youths in savage barter:
one Asian on a bike, one
white with post-punk
haircut, eyes bold with
Anglo-Saxon entitlement.

Ah, how different this
from public-schooled,
soft southern-accented
scenes on BBC television
with multi-hued 'kids'
united in youth against
everyone over thirty.

How different this from
tired Blue Peter, with its
strident cod-consensus
from postwar Neverland
and 'Rah-Rah' monarchism
from recently-suspected
middle-aged presenters.

No blue-jeaned hipsters
telling Jackanory tales
nor Bagpuss drowsing
among antiques on that
quiet street. The bike
swapped owners: this
was a different world.

Yessica Klein
Here, Daffodils

crown & crack the mulch open –
        their sun pops
        & the chest reawakens
        with a Latin American hair-flip

there,
        them clumps of pre-summer promises
        are owned by ipês in the end of August –
        before the real summer melts the tarmac rug

there –
        the city you loved, the language you left
        green & yellow umbilical chord nicknamed saudade –
        but motherland's hearts are malleable

            here, here –

these daffodils –
        eight years to rewrite a home –
        set them Latino sobs free
        & smile, inner child, smile

Phil Knight
The Public Benefactor: And Why His Statue Should Not Have Fallen

I know he was a "controversial" figure.
And I feel sorry for the people whose
Planet got blown up. Some say they had
It coming, but I am not one of them.

But we honestly have to face facts.
The Emperor Palpatine had his good points,
he provided thousands of jobs on lots of planets
by building Death Stars. People forget that.

And the space shuttles always ran on time.
This new lot in power cannot even complete
The hyperspace by-pass between Terra Prime
And Arrakis. That is vital to galactic trade.

Yes, what happened to the younglings was awful.
But you cannot judge the past by the standards
Of the present. It was a different back then.
Things must be seen in their historical context.

He was standing up to clerical extremism.
If it was not for Palpatine the whole galaxy
Would have been a Theocracy. Religious Law!
Or worst Robots would be in charge now.

We will need a strong man like that if
The Daleks or the Cylons come calling.
Not that I am defending his excesses, but
He also had a lot of bad people around him.

You see we cannot just cancel history.
It had happened. Learn to live with it.
Tearing down his statues was pointless.
Not that I am one of them First Order types, but...

Jennifer Langer
In England's Green and Pleasant Land

the god Morpheus sings to them   the *Black Rabbit* pub revellers
drunk on the English landscape of long ago -
the fields that ooze of high summer
the woods dark with secrets
the grey castle in the distance on the hill
the river shimmying along with its bouquet of sea smells

in the city   in the labyrinth of night upon night
they sleep on cruel concrete
swaddled like mummies outside Heals
mocked by mattresses in the window
they dream of sand as soft as silk
but fear the hands of midnight wanderers

at the *Black Rabbit* joy upon joy hangs in the sunlight
moored boats drift   sleepy in the reeds
weeping willow bows to the river
women's dresses float   delicate as petals
colonial chairs enfold the diners bursting with
laughter, battered fish, sticky toffee pudding, tanglewood pie

outside the tube station a man squats like a buddha
and the marching feet of apathy stride by his shadow
a woman's hand creeps down from a conch shell against a foreboding sky
and a box of left-over biscuits drops in his lap
and the loudspeaker orders people to obey it
keep away from beggars   give to homeless charities it insists

the river is indifferent and yet it murmurs but
the trees of the woods sometimes moan in anguish

Zahira P Latif
The British Way

Beliefs about a meritocratic British society were prevalent among international students from the global South during my postgraduate studies. Stereotypes of a fair and just British society were juxtaposed against their nations with their underdeveloped economies and nepotistic and corrupt societies.

Those from less affluent backgrounds undertook employment.

When that job they thought they were qualified for went to a less experienced British white student, they began to see an unfair Britain.

On highlighting issues of discrimination, the response from the white middle-class faculty was a rather condescending, "You must be mistaken, because that is not the British way".

Charles G Lauder, Jr
Into the Home Office, 10AM

Cerberus stands at the top of the long,
narrow stairs funnelling claimants in ones
and twos, its three heads barking, foaming
at all who dare ascend, snakes protruding
from its hulk peer deep into the eyes
of a Nigerian doctor, a Jamaican student,
inspecting for deceit and scroungers,
thin tiny tongues whip a bit of venom
into the faces of a Brazilian mother
and her teenage daughters
before they reach the top step
so that no one walks taller than Cerberus.
And then its python tail, barring any escape
and curled around a heavy handle, pulls on it:
Through that door! Through that door!
to an airless, supplicant-ridden room.
When the Indian couple in front of me
are ordered *through that door* I glimpse,
slunk in the corner, Moussa, a teacher
from the Ivory Coast who makes the pizzas
where I wait tables, cash in hand, no questions.
I expect the same snarling, snapping, fate,
the odoriferous breath of those multitude
of mouths that hollows out souls as they climb.
But Cerberus's crush of eyes centers on me
and soften, the snakeheads retreat,
the dogheads quietly pant,
as Cerberus settles back on its haunches,
its python tail a gentle beat against the floor.
Where am I going? To file for residency
(like everyone else). Cerberus smiles
and ushers me *through this door,*
into a hushed, less crowded waiting room
where I have no problem finding a seat.
The clerk who takes and stamps my forms
with approval, but never summons me

86

to interview, is the last official I ever see,
as if I've subdued them all with a wooden club
or just a lion-skin shield.

E B Lipton
Welcome Stranger

Welcome to our dreary shores, to unsmiling skies
Sad summers and unending winter whine.
Welcome to commuter crowds and hostile looks
To costly rooms, torn lino, cracked windows
To shared loos, damp walls, absent landlords
Welcome to our multi-lingual, multi-cultural Babel
To loneliness, lack of family and friendships
To centres, immigration, job, detention, housing, medical
Centres, where distrust and documents abound
And red tape entangles, strangles,
Welcome to waiting rooms of patient patients
To classrooms, papered walls with brown-edged pictures
Where children learn to forget their mother tongue.
Welcome.

Rob Lowe
For The Good of Our Country

For the good of our country
We murder others,
Close borders
On the needy.

For the good of our country
We defend
Our right to be right to the end
And know that others are wrong.

For the good of our country
We tell lies,
Do not love our neighbours
For they might be our enemies

For the good of our country

For the good of our country
We preserve
An imagined way of life
As if it were solid and real.

For the good of our country
We believe in religion,
Loyalty, zeal
And all the other shields

That hide us from the truth
For the good of our country
We go to war and kill.

Jacob Lund
Another National Portrait

Assuming that the night staff were Provos,
The Brigadier was framed, gilt of Clozapine
like a bullseye mirror, though thin,
cyanotype to eyes but his, and grey
so far as understanding was concerned.
Otherwise, he wasn't alone at all:
his histories mimed away at ours in
illusory discourses under glass;
light dust as fixity.

Backgrounding, lucid, ageless as old dark,
we put ourselves, him, onto a watch
perspectival as a kind of love that is
not quite enough,
where our captions are obscured
though new-named, changed beneath all recognition,
alive on a paint-rich square of wall.

We, faux-strangers, pass in front of those
who cannot leave, which is to see that
vacated rooms have open doors still not
internalised, our legends confused
as far as all available exits.

Jacob Lund
The Gift Shop by the Sea

Here are little *Hakenkreuze*
for excitable Englishmen, watched by
Dönitz and Jodl,
peering nervously,
lying yellow, stiff
from the smell of Bovril on the *Sketch*,
silent as the orchestras of bakelite.

From below you can watch the bunting flap
its forced emblems as it choruses down the pier
to the closed epoch, where at the beachhead
crouch the invisible boys, the overlords,
their avatars looking for a ruck with themselves,
as if that is to fight.

What some of us say we know is only half true:
the rest lies static between the stations,
between the microphone and the desire
where the human sits,
examining its archives on thick paper.

Jacob Lund
Old Words

Fully inert, we hear them
true as Saxon axes,
blunt comforters for those
among us in need of a straight story:
logorrheic if need be;
wept over if it must.

Lethality should not be
underestimated, where
the accountants and the postmen
dress up and cry for Godwinson,
mutter about fun over ale,
whet blades for themselves,
for the old words, and later

was it someone English who said
that language and thought went –
not with condemned hands, perhaps –
but inseparably? No matter:
there's an execution cemetery
making all that noise.

Walid Marmal
Fur and Furlough

I want to follow the rules and stay home
and ease off the pressure on the NHS
But… Alas! … I don't have a home
I only have a cabin, or less.

Social distancing is my status quo
since I've got no family or friends
every day I just go with the flow
and wait to meet my ends.

This draconian system has torn me down
and left my soul dull and arid
now I can't care less about the lockdown
or all the fuss about covid.

Living on thirty-seven pounds a week
is the memory of the good old days
now I have no allowance to seek
like a church-mouse which erratically strays.

My summer shoes are damp and old
and charity shops have shut their doors
three pairs of socks won't halt the cold
nor the frostbite that numbs my toes.

I wish to have a fur coat and fur shoes
a house, a kitchen with lots of dough
and on some weekends make barbecues
and be like those with "fur and furlough".

This poem was written in 2020 during lockdown when I was living in a wooden cabin in the garden
of an acquaintance's house. My asylum application had been rejected and I was thus denied any
kind of accommodation or allowance.

Fokkina McDonnell
In Blighty

So much here in Blighty has been lost, replaced, or deleted: in the
grey city centre European Christmas markets confront an accumulation
of dirty duvets in doorways of offices and hotels. I hear the faint ticking of
clocks, hold memories of closed libraries, swimming pools. No seconds
are offered in foodbanks. Minutes after my friend put tinned rice in
a cardboard box in Sainsbury's, she tripped on the cracked pavement which
has an outline in white paint. *The people,* many of them, dream of empires
returning. The past was always another country and pipe dreams are
made of clay. One man's dream is another woman's nightmare. I was born
in a land below the sea, the North Sea, a country where politicians gather
around tables, walk the corridors in The Hague to arrive, eventually, at their
destination: consensus, compromise, through *polderen.* I cry at the height
of hypocrisy when *Britannia rules the waves, Jerusalem,* and
other iconic symbols are stolen by those monied men who have now become
European citizens simply through buying in. The UK, my home for 48 years, is broken
but the chimneys of empty factories will outlive the stately statues
of proud admirals on horseback. They are already covered in pigeon shit and
some wear a fluorescent yellow jacket. High up in the Gallery are Victorian friezes
and dusty glass cases display the relics of civilisation, while upstairs in
the *Elgin Room* a silent queue shuffles, some people are crying. These museums,
(yes, every town or city has its *Museum of Lost Marbles),* have at the far
end the emergency exit, a green man running, running, running away.

A Golden Shovel poem inspired by a line from "Nine Allegories of Power", by John Siddique: 'The accumulation
of seconds in which empires are born, gather their height and become broken statues and friezes in museums
far away.'

The last word of each line in "In Blighty" make the line I borrowed from Siddique's poem.

Fokkina McDonnell
Going bananas
An abecedarian poem

Aliens' Office: the first destination on my 1969 arrival, a somewhat
bewildering encounter with Blighty's bureaucracy in London.
Colombey-les-Deux-Églises it ain't and I'm in Manchester now, five
decades down the timeline, feeling like a sick parrot, a dead one
even. I was an economic migrant, attracted by English eccentricity.
Four candles? Fork handles? Wit and humour have been turned into the
Groundhog Day of Brexit negotiations. Jack took a fortnight's leave -
halcyon days in September - and through marriage I acquired an
Irish surname while my husband held two passports, even then.
Je ne regrette rien screech those who voted *non* in the referendum.
Kafka would have been enchanted by a hard border in the Irish sea.
Languages were my passport, small flags sewn on the uniforms;
my Seaman's Record Book rests in a box file with birthday cards.
NHS nurses and paediatricians are returning to Europe, even poets I know.
Oui, some of the three million are voting with their feet.
P&O gave the world the word *posh:* port out, starboard home. The
question of lorries queueing on the M20 still has no answer, as do the
refugee tales of children held in indefinite detention or stuck in Calais.
Schadenfreude is not what they feel in Europe, they're just bewildered.
Tourist shoppers avail themselves of the sinking pound sterling and the
ugly UKIP man with Union Jack footwear, beery bonhomie, claimed
victory then scarpered sharply right. What kind of victory is it
when I now no longer want to become a British citizen? My neighbours are
xenophobes who, Macron says, will soon need visit visa to enter France.
Yes, the yahoos are among us yanking us closer and closer to the edge,
zealots who prefer the zilch-no-deal, while I cry and pluck my zither.

Fokkina McDonnell
Britain

Britain is a homburg hat
that will produce a rabbit
if you ask nicely.

This country is a parking ticket
on a rainy day: bright yellow
with small, smudged writing.

Britain is an apple, stolen
or fallen from an unkempt tree:
not enough to make a wholesome pie.

Nicollen Meek
She's never had it so good

At a party, she yelled back
"The Prime Minister wouldn't lie -
That's lefty conspiracy."
Winter came and coffins piled
"It wasn't his fault the pandemic struck."
Voices were crushed, protesters arrested
Vulnerable abandoned, human rights abuse inflicted
"Governments all over the world make hard decisions.
I agree no one should suffer, but that's unrealistic."

Children went hungry, teenagers stripped,
Workers lost jobs as profits increased
Bonuses swelled, nurses denied leave.
Anti-racism paper patted the backs of the whites
As the privilege and wealth gap grew wide
"We're better than America. Have you tried being more grateful?"

War blew in, no room for national disasters
The oak of social security reduced to a toothpick.
Nothing to spare, tips on how to spend less
"My grandparents never spent money on a fancy TV,
It's about time people knew how little they need."

The pantomime erupted, tickets to its show costing lives
Journalists and entertainers mocking the audience
Of citizens and immigrants, the very life blood of these times,
Pitting deniers against the denied,
Reminding us that Brexit got done -
"Look how the miners came to an end,
Don't put your children's future in a striker's will to stand."

But then came her line. One she could not ignore.
"My national insurance will be too high, my bills are a scream,
I have holiday plans abroad,
It's time to put an end to this war
Against me and what I deserve."

And with the fever of a gambler, she rallied for house-win
Betting on the other side of the same coin, she was sure was worthy.
The sure thing.

And as the bloodied baton passed,
from one prison ward to the next,
she loosened her purse, she clinked her glass
"See, it's always worth fighting for a better end."

Nicollen Meek
The friends of my enemies sleep well

A leopard has as many spots as it has as many friends,
No more so than the leopard lounging in St James's Den.

For leopard finds its friends good company to keep
Providing compliments and bones to clean their bloody teeth,
So when the herd begins its scavenging for the day
Leopard's breath won't reek of the lives it took away.

As for the herd, they believe there is safety in their numbers
But numbers are what friends fill leopard's pockets in abundance.

Even though the prey can sense the danger in its predator
The friends have built systems of apathetic surrender
Undermining lives with lies of freedom from starvation and suffering.
A half-eaten carrot is always better than nothing.

And when the friends begin to out stay their welcome
The leopards are ready to pounce and pin the problem
On the herd, mice like masters of their own demise,
How could anyone bring prosperity to these greedy, sickly, lives.
They should be grateful the leopards have friends willing to invest
To guide, and deliver self-efficient cattle markets
Whose offshore success made everyone a winner.
There's no nobler cause than sacrificing a few for leopard's dinner.

For the friends of leopard are nothing more than poachers
Whose trophy is their hoard of wealth, education, culture and shelter
Because who would leopard's friends be, without our eradication
How would their friends eat, without our starvation
What would their friends do, without our unemployment
When would their friends gain, without our debasement.

Jenny Mitchell
Lowfields, Jamaica

A thinning man in a hospice bed
has to use his whole frame, his whole mind
to answer the question, *Where do you live?*
Slowly he says, *Lowfields, Jamaica.*

I know he's lived in England for over fifty years.
He came as a boy who helped his father
gather the cane. It blooms on the top
when it's time to cut down, so he tells me.

I hear a rattling sound when he speaks –
the duppies have taken his lungs. He remembers
the time he dared his kid brother to climb
on the roof of the Colony Club, reserved for the whites.

He unhooked the Union Jack and waved it
above his head in triumph.
The constable beat him into the jail,
beat him till his eyes were closed.

His left arm was never the same again.
He refused to sing *God Save the Queen*
in school after that and was caned for refusing.
Lowfields, Jamaica – yes.

He came as a boy who helped his father
gather the cane. It blooms on the top
when it's time to cut down, so he tells me.
It blooms on the top when it's time to cut down.

Colleen Molloy
Dolphins

There were six people in the boat
He was the only survivor
Each time the waves pushed him under
They brought him to the surface
He thought they would eat him
The terrors of the sea woke him up every night for years
Until he understood they'd saved his life.

Helen Moore
Approaching Britain, Snapshots 2017

Our faces honeyed moons   in the glass of Eurostar
        as we careen by vast, bleak fields
of global agribusiness…. (7ᵗʰ October, newlyweds returning from Paris.)

        Before Calais-Fréthun, train slows past long   kilometres
of razor wire –   a concentration built to keep
        the 'migrants' out.   Not a soul

                21ˢᵗ January, from Ethiopia, Johnsina, 20,
                struck dead by a truck near Calais

in sight, except high atop   a fence
        a Thrush   unfazed by wheel-knives' whine,
the blast of air   below.
                2ⁿᵈ May, a person (age, gender, origin unknown),
                electrocuted atop the roof of a train bound for London

        Here's an unromantic view of Europe –   & Britain
with its *Lien Vital*   through which goods & chattels
        shuttle   to & fro.

                * 22ⁿᵈ December, from Afghanistan, Abdullah Dilsouz, 15,*
                killed by a lorry on a road near Calais

In the dark, under-sea tunnel   (leased from Charon)
        senses are engulfed   as panic-bubbles burst
in random flashes, and   *(Could that've been?)*   a face

                * 27ᵗʰ December, from Eritrea, a man aged 31*
                crushed in a truck when it crashed near Calais

        looking   in –   someone fleeing
from the whipping hands of war / torture / famine,
        someone who's   somehow
                                getting through?

29th December, from Afghanistan, Jabar
died in a truck near Calais, trying to join siblings in Britain

Etc, etc, etc

---

*From the UNITED List of Deaths, 1/4/2019, documenting 36,570 deaths of refugees & migrants due to the restrictive policies of 'Fortress Europe', (such as border closures, asylum laws, accommodation, detention policies, deportations, carrier sanctions), which date back to 1993. The list, which is updated annually, can be freely re-used, translated & re-distributed, provided the source is cited: www.unitedagainstracism.org

Hubert Moore
Collisions

I still keep voices of small boats
especially of punts and rowing-boats
softly colliding with each other
in my head. These days collisions
happen much more angrily. It seems
our Threatforce wants a not
too public way of pushing boats
they don't approve of back
across the sea. I hope they don't
use poles like those we used to stir
up mud-clouds as we pushed
our lovers up and down the river
in a punt. These orange-jacketed
arrivers bring their own home
voices with them in their heads,
their soft collisions. A sloping beach
growls at them as they land.

Hubert Moore
Demonic

'Pandemonium', the pest-controller
said when he'd finished
pumping poison in the nest
the wasps had built, 'That'll be
pandemonium in there.'
And yes I guess we're all of us
in there, every people-pandering
demon you can think of, demons
who chose to kill a city
and demons on screens we must
have somehow nodded to
who send survivors back
to pandemonium, into the ruins
of their poisoned city.

KE Morash
Foreigner

I'm
not from here.
But you knew that,
didn't you?
You can tell just by looking.
My physique is sleek. I'm tall, angular, if I dare say,
more comely than standard domestic fare:
all low and squat and entirely- expected.
Still, to you, I'm awkward; no   WI- crafted
cozy accommodates my   alien shape.
It's fine! I keep myself warm in   this cool climate.
I'm from away. You can tell just by   listening. Music
pours from my mouth, her prologue to   breakfast;
a pre-biscuit overture. It's true, I have   taken the job
of a native-born, who sits dusty and neglected in
a dank space. But in me, she sees her reflection,
my cobalt nazars swirling energy against evil eyes.
(she's foreign too). You can tell by touch. Her hand
fits perfectly to contours born for pouring. In me,
she feels potential; I could—if she desired—serve
beverages hot OR cold. Could an English pot
do that? It could not. Dare I say it? I do.
In me, the tea simply tastes
better.

106

Chris Morley
Pointless Packaging

Shrink wrapped food just makes me mad
It's the worst idea that we've ever had
A heat sealed swede isn't what we need
We haven't thought where this will lead

Food comes packed in its plastic trays
Together with cardboard overlays
Tell me what is wrong with a paper bag
It's all that my Granny ever had

Chorus

Banana's already got a skin
We don't need a wrapper to put it in
Nevertheless we keep making a mess
With our endless pointless packaging

Too much packaging so much waste
We throw away what we buy in haste
How many bags have you thrown away
Five hundred years 'till they decay

Moulded polystyrene won't break down
It fills up the ground and hangs around
So much plastic and cellophane
It just won't stop 'till we complain

Chorus

Banana's already got a skin
We don't need a wrapper to put it in
Nevertheless we keep making a mess
With our endless pointless packaging
Don't throw your bags away
Use them another day
Let's put an end to pointless packaging

107

Loraine Masiya Mponela
Train of Life

The man I saw on BBC News crying
in Ukraine
was a foreigner

he was told to go back
back to face Putin
as if he had invited Putin to invade the country to start with

prejudice in full glare
everyone else jumped onto the train
to flee a war they all feared
but not this man

he was not allowed to leave
as if he was a special creation
who loved war and death

They wanted a visa from him

He did not have one
and so for want of a piece of paper
his life could be sacrificed

for want of a piece of paper
he became less than human

man in a strange land
no family
no friends
carrying nothing but his life
a life worth nothing in train conductors' eyes
because he is a foreigner
expected to stay back in a land not his own
where the skies rain bombs and bullets
like he had started it all

He is not interested in this fight
will not get the spoils of this fight
does not want any part of it

all he wants is to live
and one day find home
away from a war he did not start
away from demons he did not release

Loraine Masiya Mponela
I saw my mother burn alive

I read on the internet about Andriy
a 15-year-old Ukrainian who said, *I saw my mother burn alive*
from a landmine

He saw the driver of the car he was in die
and he saw his sister die

with blood coming out of his ears
Andriy crawled away

He dreams of them every night
sees and hears their screams
even as he sits at the dining table

He can't sleep at night
because the images are too bright

when he does fall asleep the heat of the fire that killed his family
wakes him up in a sweat each night

Locked up in this private hell
he asks, *What is the purpose of life?*

Ambrose Musiyiwa
What A Wonderful War

Said energy companies to one another,
This is a wonderful war. Look at all the oil and gas we're selling. Look at
the prices they're fetching, and look at all the money we're making.

Said governments of the global North to energy companies,
We need more oil, gas and coal. Give us more oil, gas and coal.

Said the people of the global South to the global North,
This war is hurting us. Look at the food shortages and unrest it is causing.

Said the governments of the global North to the South,
Give us your oil, gas, coal and minerals. If you refuse, we'll hurt you even
more and still take what we want from you.

Said the people of the global North to their governments,
This war is affecting our comfort and eroding our wages. Look at how
much more we now have to pay for everything, for food, clothing, shelter,
and for fuel.

Said the governments of the global North to their people,
We thank you for your sacrifice.

Said the government of Ukraine to the global North,
We need more money. We need more weapons. And we need more
sanctions on Russian oil, gas and coal.

Said the global South to the North,
This is a bad, bad war. It's bad for business. It's bad for the environment,
and it's bad for humanity.

Said the governments of the global North to the South,
Stop spreading this propaganda. If you are not on our side, lockstep, lock,
stock and barrel, you are on the side of our enemies.

Ambrose Musiyiwa
These Streets Think of Summer
Leicester, 17 June 2017

we chose this place,
                    or
            this place chose us

looked at from above,
the streets around the Clock Tower
have the shape of an icicle

as angels mingle with crowds,
in the near tropical heat,
sampling continental, Mediterranean
and world dishes
at the party
            greeting new arrivals

the cooling sound and lulling spray
of water
from the fountain

i meet Venus on Horsefair Street
            she cannot stop

the families, poets, priests, lovers,
musicians and Pan
bask,
picnic in the sun,
remembering
celebrating Venus' sister, Jo

the historians, philosophers, prophets
and revolutionaries
at the cross
            pointing the way
            to the heart of the city,
prophesy a time

when money
will not be a measure
for human life

"These Streets Think of Summer" was inspired by the Continental Market that was held around the Clock Tower in Leicester on 17 June 2017; the Refugee Week celebration that was held in Town Hall Square; the event celebrating the life of Jo Cox that was held at Leicester Cathedral; and the convergence of protests that took place at Jubilee Square, all on the same day.

The poem has also been featured, written in chalk on the pavement at the Leicester Against War / Leicester for Peace vigil that took place at the Clock Tower weekly from late 2015 until about late 2019. The vigil was the longest running vigil of its kind in Leicester. Among other things, the vigil was calling for an end to British military intervention in countries like Syria and on Britain to do more to support people seeking refuge.

113

Andy N
Turning against Prejudices

If the war between Russia and Ukraine
had happened in the 17th century
would people fleeing from the war zone
have been grabbed by slavers
and packed head to tail
over the black sea in their boats

Would they have been auctioned,
sent to chop cane, pick cotton
beat until the shell of their lives
were left as traces in the wind
over Liverpool, Bristol and Glasgow

Would they still be cargo jettisoned
or left to starve;
their spirits haunting the sea
for hundreds of years afterwards
threaded with helplessness
floating in a cul-de-sac of generations,

floating in changing landscapes
opening up our doors
for families left with nothing
turning against prejudices
that ruled previous lifetimes

Nasrin Parvaz
Black bird

Which of these thousands
                    of standing stones
                    engraved with a black number
                                        belongs to you?

            Stones
                        as white as a bride's dress
                                    you never wore.

You were a black bird
                    caught by men
                                your father
                                            or brother
who plucked your feathers
                            one
                                    by
                                            one
throughout your life
                        before
                                    slashing your throat.

Nasrin Parvaz
Acting

It must had been his first day of begging
he was clean and good looking
standing, rather than sitting
he took a step or two towards the passers by
smiling and asking politely for spare change.
I mistook him for George Clooney, acting
in one of his Hollywood films.
I imagined him afterwards
washing himself thoroughly
in one of his glass showers
in one of his mansions
that could house hundreds of beggars.

Leonie Philip
Pain

We travelled from the Caribbean all dressed up.
Looking for streets paved with gold.
Choose any job you like because they said so.
Get work and a room for you and the family.

At Waterloo station with your battered valise.
Waiting on platform two for Cousin Joyce.
In the distance you see her waving.
A broad smile and bright brown eyes gleaming.

At 91 Brook Street a tiny room awaits you.
Old stove, broken sink, food cabinet all dirty and greasy.
The bed creaks un-balance one wheel off.

Next day work at the Biscuit Factory.
Three and sixpence a week, shilling for the rent.
Another shilling for food, two and sixpence for box money and fares.

You marry Johnny have children in this tiny room.
You get home late, cook, eat, you half asleep, still Johnny wants night food.
You find yourself pregnant, child number six.

Back street abortion, one and two, ask God to forgive you,
Johnny gone and left you; you struggle with the children, more worries.
You look for bigger rooms, no blacks, no Irish, no dogs; you are not
    welcome here.

Children grown up, gone their own way.
Leaving you and stepfather to be alone.
Worry about where life have gone.
Several years later back to the Caribbean.
Fulfilling the dream, home larger than you neighbours; with servant,
    gardener, and all.
Life have come full circle to what you knew.
You are treated like a foreigner by your own.
In the course of time; they do not fit in.

117

The homeland has changed, modernity overtaken them.
Go back to England where there is no gold.
The returners are the strangers, their health depleted.
Back to the homeland; only to find free bus pass and medicine.
All the other free things you get.
When you look back, it is better to be here.
No going back, old friends are still here, will die here.

I am not going back; I will stay here for my children
and grandchildren along with the pain I bear.

Natasha Polomski
Pity the Nation
A Tribute to Lawrence Ferlinghetti, For Britain

Pity the{nation}whose history is silenced
whose identity is bound up in lies
whose criminals are protected
and discontents locked up
and whose rules silence only the wise.
Pity the{nation}that sings only for itself
who knows nothing but its own blurred reflection
Who is immune to the truth
and deaf to the cries
of those who speak out with conviction.
Pity the{nation}who exports weapons for profit
who seeks glory through bombing campaigns,
who fights terror with terror
mines wealth by dispossession
and laughs at its own body's demise.
And pity its people
who eat up its lies
and blind themselves to their own error
Who ask for their own downfall,
and cheer as it happens,
Oh Jerusalem,
tears I shall cry.

steve pottinger
Swallows

when the swallows arrived
next spring
we were ready

with paperwork, permits, and protocols
with questions and with quotas
forms filled in, in triplicate, by hatchet-faced clerks

with suspicion, without sentiment
and speeches from our government
about the need to keep our country safe
from those from foreign parts

swallows found flying into the country at night
were shipped back to the continent
wings clipped, in chains
citizens with swallows' nests on their property
were fined, named, shamed
if the traffic was bad
or the trains were late
the swallows were blamed

while politicians railed
and there was gloating in the press
our skies were emptier, quieter
our summer less blessed
each morning we were reminded
that we had been saved from
the unspeakable machinations and evils
of swallows

and we taught ourselves to understand
this was for the best

steve pottinger
Moving on

wave goodbye to solidarity,
xenophobia's in vogue
jackboots are just so passé,
let's vote for stylish brogues
who needs angry demagogues?
we're a pair of raffish rogues
the cheeky charming chancers
we've moved on

we used to hate the blacks and irish,
now it's albanians and poles
we've learned to use the glottal stop,
and patronise the proles
and we've privatised the contract for the bloke
who digs the holes
deeper deeper deeper
we've moved on

don't try and set events in context,
the past is best forgotten
the system works to our advantage,
while we tell you that it's rotten
we blame the foreigners, the unemployed,
the poor folk at the bottom
does that all sound a bit familiar?
let's move on

the power that dropped into our hands,
we didn't quite expect it
the siren songs of sovereignty
has led us all to brexit
by the time you get your country back,
there's every chance we will have wrecked it
and while you're picking up the pieces
we'll move on
a simple slogan in a complex world,

we want our country back
the fist that masquerades as bumbling
is still a weapon that attacks
a foolish flag-wrapped falsehood
flying in the face of facts
you'd think by now we should know better

moving on

steve pottinger
England

Straight off the bat let me say
I was never a fan
I mean don't speak ill and all that
but if we're clearing the decks
wiping the slate clean
getting it all out in the open
then...
you were bloody hard work, England,
not easy to live with, let alone love.

You see, you kept making me and my friends
sit cricket tests I was never going to pass
took our taxes and our labour
but still left us feeling second class
because our roots stretched back
to other cultures, other shores
and other teams made our guilty, secret hearts
beat a little faster, race a little more.
Even now, it's like you can't help yourself
some scoundrel starts waving the flag
critical thought goes out of the window
and next thing you know
you've tanked yourself up on bigotry and lager
giving it *'2 world wars and 1 world cup'*
like you fired the winning shot yourself.
I mean really, England? Really?
I've seen you running for the bus
in the mornings, and it's not pretty.
You're a heart attack waiting to happen
hypertension, clogged arteries, dodgy knees
it's all history, for fuck's sake
do yourself a favour, let it go.

And you were the chink of fine china
the tyranny of manners and the old school tie

tut-tut-tutting about the enemy within
turning a blind eye while someone
did your dirty work
gratuitous truncheons
battles in beanfields
cover-ups and never-challenged lies.
So, like I say, it wasn't the best of starts.
I had to leave to learn to love you
get far enough away to see both sides
of the coins in your pocketful of shrapnel
find the fist that promised *'love'*
not just the one that offered *'hate'*.

And out there,
on the other side of the world
I found I missed you
missed your dirt under my fingernails
hankered after your way with words
your dirty laugh
your seaside postcard humour
and your beautiful mongrel language.
Every time you open your mouth
history tumbles from your lips
in dialect and accent
a pulsing archaeology of trade
invasion, conquest, immigration
the ebb and flow of populations
making room making homes
and getting assimilated
learning there's precious few of life's problems
not cut down to size with another cup of tea
and a couple of biccies.

You're not dead.
You're just evolving
re-inventing yourself
getting your nails done
putting on your glad rags
for a night out on the town

and I will find you
on top of the moors
quoting Benny Hill and Shakespeare
feasting on samosas and flagons of cider
slapping the taut drum of your stomach
where it spills over the waistband of your trousers
– *all paid for, kid!* –
proud as punch
Falstaff, as I live and breathe
paddling in the shallows
beyond the deckchairs and the donkeys
giggling in Gujerati
the hem of your sari trailing in the cold North Sea
salty and wet while your wide-eyed kids
play shoot-em-up in the arcades
mither you for fish and chips
support City and United
and ride the bus home
with their heads full of dreams
knowing love triumphs
over cricket tests every time
and their hearts beat
proud and strong.

Matteo Preabianca
A flag dilemma

Propaganda rhymes with panda
which has something in common with British democracy:
almost extinct! Endangered!

I land in the UK at the wrong time:
pandemic, Brexit, war, inflation.

The first is China's fault, said that guy without a comb, and now without
    a job.
The second is the EU's fault, said that guy seated in that parliament for
    twenty years,
dreaming of leaving the poor Europeans.

The third is the Russian elite's fault.
"How did they pay for their UK properties?" said another guy sitting in
    Westminster.

And the fourth one? Everybody's fault. It's also my fault!

British news are so biased and childish:
Putin bad, Zelenskyy good.
Meanwhile let's keep quiet and welcome to Britain as many oligarchs as we
    can.
Such a jubilee of rubles!

"A sovereign country can decide which side it stands on,"
 said again the guy with Highland cow hair.

I walked around my town. Every window, every garden has a Ukrainian
    flag.
A good business for the ignorant!

I have never seen an Iraqi flag, nor an Afghan one.
But, you know, they don't sell them in TK Maxx.
I want to buy a Russian flag. But they told me Russia is bad.
Wait till the gas comes to its end.

Then we will make amends.

"The enemies are at my gate," the warrior said.
"Bullshit!" replied Grandpa Sam,
and Sweden plus Finland, welcome to the club.

Welcome Ukrainian refugees!
But if you are Black – please...

I am just a stupid foreigner in this land,
but why will you make me a citizen for more than a grand?

mona rae
After the Ofsted Visit

The safeguarding lead makes a racist 'joke'
But 'isn't racist'
Still, he runs Prevent trainings

Oblivious to the bigotry
Of lonely, white boys from remote, rural areas
Who are groomed as they game

Regurgitating 'banter'
Into overcrowded classrooms
Unchallenged by chill teachers

Who did not hear any racist accents
Or sexist anecdotes
As they dead-named through roll call

The white, cisgender diversity officer
Doesn't like conflict
And doesn't have time

Another cancelled meeting
Another resignation
Another drop-out

The pastoral manager dismisses students
Between mocking masks
And switching off ventilation

While the principal threatens expulsion
Against the rising costs of transport
And the immediate need of housing

EHCP learners
'Learning' how to take exams
And what to say to Ofsted

Who can't visualise a future
Complete with kitchen renovations
On an empty stomach

Budget cuts and broken equipment
Busy work and British values
Build Back Better

The only other staff of colour
Tells me to keep my head down
And to jump through the hoops

But I am here to take up space

And context is key
In a Tory-run school
Chaired by the Prime Minister's brother

EHCP: An Education, Health and Care (EHC) Plan is for children and young people aged up to 25 who need more support than is available through special educational needs support.

Ofsted: The Office for Standards in Education. A non-ministerial department that inspects services providing education and skills for learners of all ages.

British Values: Section 78 of the Education Act 2022 requires schools to promote pupils' spiritual, moral, social and cultural development. This includes promoting the fundamental British values of democracy, the rule of law, individual liberty, and mutual respect and tolerance of those with different faiths and beliefs.

Prevent: The aim of Prevent is to tackle the causes of radicalisation and respond to the ideological challenge of terrorism; safeguard and support those most at risk of radicalisation through early intervention; and enable those who have already engaged in terrorism to disengage and rehabilitate.

Source of definitions: https://www.gov.uk/ Accessed 29 March 2023

S Reeson
End Times in Fortress Britain

In the end, nobody cares.

We are already a dystopia, the End Times
sneaking in between Love Island and the News,
as a Muppet Government instructs us all, each one
to go stand in direct sun, as temperatures
exceed forty degrees, proving that Brits
not afraid of some ridiculous scuttlebutt
that their World is burning to the ground.

Cute delivery robots are deployed
as millions starve, rely on food banks,
handouts: millions more, if they survive
the heat are just as likely then to freeze
first moment Summer leaves, but no-one
seems to care about these things as long
as likes and followers remain intact.

Good luck selling this to anyone as news
they'd all rather publish avant-garde
or keep recycling same old tosh
recalling green and pleasant stans
a history, no longer theirs to hold
the final days of Empire, banned,
quiet, white bred evolution, crumbling.

Why is nobody listening to us.

Marilyn Ricci
Her Afro

frames clever brown eyes,
auburn hints at the tip of each curl.
In a school of mainly white kids
many like to touch: *Oooh, so soft!*

Mostly she allows it but today, on her way
from English to History, her hand rises:
No, she says. *No more.*

Marilyn Ricci
Double History

Today they're doing slavery.
She flicks back her braids, studies
the list, gasps at seeing her surname.

When Miss isn't looking, googles
and a massive mansion appears built
with compensation for their loss of 'property'.

Her body becomes still. Waits to fathom:
her mother not managing on seventy pounds a week,
the whispering man on the street: *Go home.*

Kay Ritchie
Naming

(Invera Estate, Tobago
120 enslaved men, women & children
value of estate - £13,862
value of people - £4,689)

They say I'm 34. I was a child when they transported me from an Igbo kingdom far away and paid for me in beads although they say I'm worth more than the others. They named me Peggy the first, for they have no imagination, these plantation owners who possess two other Peggy's, two Penny's, two Hettie's, two Rosean's. They tell me I'm black, Creole and healthy but we're all bound in chains, physically, mentally. And their Holy Bible, brought all the way from London, 'for the use of negro slaves in British west Indian islands' has tortured truth, boiled down liberty, mercy, justice, as we boil down their sugar cane. And the proceeds of our forced labour leaves us for some distant land called Glasgow where 'improved streets' are named Jamaica, Virginia, Tobago, for they have no imagination, these plantation owners and we are mere inventory.

Kay Ritchie
Theft

these are not my heroes
these Glasgow merchants
who name our streets
Cunninghame   Cochrane
Buchanan   Ingram
Glassford   Oswald   Spiers
their fortunes made
in the triangle trade
that 'Let Glasgow Flourish'

first they stole the people
then they stole the history
of Africa's Sierra Leone
so every stone   every street
stinks of blood   sweat   bone
no name or place or date of birth recorded
only the numbers   the ages   the costs
of these nameless we should celebrate
whose anonymous toil on West Indian soil
made the fortunes of those we commemorate
who are not my heroes

Caroline Rooney
Welcome

Welcome to England!

Wide welcome to our green and pleasant pastures,
Their stately homes white as cotton, white as sugar.

Welcome to Heathrow!

We look forward to being your hottest seasonal
Destination as our summers become sizzlers.

Welcome to the City of London!

We offer tax cuts for the rich and offshore sharks
From logo'd banks near where the chartered Thames does flow.

Welcome to our caring country!

We host a National Health Service, though
Our ambulances can't always manage the load.

Welcome to our caring country!

We boast detention centres, or else flights
To lands remote from our moated communities.

Welcome to Westminster!

Behold our flickering democracy, while
You can't seem to vote in the leader you dream of.

Welcome to Whitehall!

We'll sell y'all weapons for the wars of the day,
Since the military industry is our mainstay.
Welcome to Fleet Street!

Here papers recycle populist prejudice
To refuel the politics of divide and rule.

Welcome to our country!

For we claim that the values of fairness and fun
And freedom are specially ours, not universal.

And still, welcome to Britain!

Stomping ground for rebels, revolutionaries:
Blue plaques for Marx, Garvey, Pankhurst and Wilde.

Mandy Ross
Human Journeys

Whispered chant:
Long ago – around the world – all of history – and today –
On the move – leaving home – don't look back – away, away –
A safe place – a strange land – make a home – journey's end.

Chorus:
Share a song of human journeys,
Over land and over sea,
From near or far, we sing together
Songs of home in Hope Street.

What could make you leave your home,
Language, people, all you know?
If you're hungry, or in danger?
Choosing hope, or forced to go?

Chorus:
Share a song of human journeys,
Over land and over sea,
From near or far, we sing together
Songs of home in Hope Street.

Some were chained. Some have passports.
Some bought tickets. Some have none.
On foot, by cart or boat or plane,
Goodbye, across the border, on.

Chorus:
Share a song of human journeys,
Over land and over sea,
From near or far, we sing together
Songs of home in Hope Street.

From faraway, the bird migrates
Without a map, flying free.

Knows no border, needs no ticket,
Builds a nest in Hope Street.

Chorus:
Share a song of human journeys,
Over land and over sea,
From near or far, we sing together
Songs of home in Hope Street.

"Human Journeys" by Mandy Ross, is song lyrics for Royal Liverpool Philharmonic Orchestra's March 2022 school concerts, which were set to orchestral music composed by Ian Stephens. The song was learned and sung in a series of concerts by over 10,000 schoolchildren, accompanied by their city's orchestra, in the Philharmonic Hall in Hope Street, Liverpool.

Hastie Salih
Privilege

My wobbly wings are set to fly,
The moon peers tearfully through the ashen sky.
My metallic heart is chipped with remorse
This flight by my airline 'Privilege' was not my intended course.

Screaming bombs pierce into foreign soil, surrounding a fight,
Setting buildings and humans alight.
Yet, when these victims try to escape,
From drought or genocide, they are denied empathy, a shape.

Forced to board me, Boeing 767, I become a mere shadow of truth,
My resentment sticks to the tarmac as I observe a youth,
Transfixed by the scars on his wrist,
His eyes wide and frozen, his hand forming a fist.

A call comes hurtling through – it seems
The European Court of Human Rights has intervened!
A security guard leaps up, the young refugee weeps
Even though on different levels, they embrace, for this is more than a
    court case.

Chrys Salt
My Welcome

I will wait on a bright rangoli
to greet you,
dried meats and fruit laid out on coloured linen
with vegetables, black tea, warm loaves
and a little salt.

I will meet you in lorries, on platforms,
on runways, on coasts, cold quays,
islands and stony beaches.

If I stick out my tongue
it is to show you it is not black
like that of the cruel king in your stories.

If I open my hands
it is not to steal your papers.
If I show you a knife
it is only to cut your meat.
My sun
will not steal your rivers.
My fire,
will not burn your wheat.

You shall have my seat at the table
with the best view of your future.

I will wade into savage waters
to save you
pull you and the ghosts of our ancestors
ashore.

Fran Sani
The Stansted Blues

I am not asleep. My eyes closed buzzing
engine uneasy landing at
Stansted airport feeling
nausea feeling sleepy
walking
out of the plane out through the gate
passport checks take a long time. For a moment
I am the latest import
in England. Imported
tea Indian Chinese
Falafel Middle
Eastern curry
Indian coffee coffee coffee
Peruvian Bolivian
Brazilian Italian pasta
Italian stocks flowing
in the city. I know
I'm hungry my luggage close to me
a sandwich at Café Nero I do not trust
the faces white brown black while I eat
one luggage I have one phone one
passport one bank card in one wallet
one jumper in the light wind the voices
tourists Italian French Spanish
American the voices at work Indian
Chinese Polish Black while I get on the
coach I squeeze in my seat. I cannot
afford the train. I know the exports of England
Chinese opium Yemenite bombs business
without nationality
business without roots
business with dividends
and a lust for the day
not to end a lust for business
a lust for work I am going to work
different the language different from English

the language at the bus
station Polish and
Spanish Hindi at the train
station different
the English I'll speak tomorrow
at my desk different Italian they
fancy stories of food of
summertime summer
gone holidays gone gone is
the day in indigo blue
in the sky on the street bikes on bikes
darker skins cheaper pants fast deliveries through the city
dark is the night my house has thin walls
many people walking in and out many flatmates.
I close myself in my room. Now I am alone.
No rain now. Rain will come tomorrow. Tomorrow
I wake up and start work. My rest starts
now my work waits for me again.

Barbara Saunders
Collections at the V&A Museum, London

Bevies of ladies envy each other's
China tea sets
No bundles of rags within these doors
Unless designer rags

Do you see this painted panel?
Knights and ladies in the foreground
With their hounds
In the distance a fleet of ships

Always in the background
The crew of sailors
The regiment of soldiers
Firing a fusillade of shots

Helping to round up people
For a gang of thieves

Barbara Saunders
Sorry

It takes longer to cross
the gap between people
than synapses.

It takes longer to stop
the man shouting abuse
at you in a silent shop.

You stand looking
at the man,
you stand shaking
your head
from a safe distance,

You turn
to your small children,
you turn your trolley
away.

No one says a word
to you, or the man.
No one says it.
Sorry.

Joel Scarfe
Picking Chit

However hot it got, the summer sun, like lava
down the narrow troughs
which in straight lines through fields would run
we'd be there, on our knees, the five of us,
each with a stack of punnets to be filled
then carried up for testing on the scales.
The nervous wait for needle to be stilled
then, if enough, down from a table made of bales
an impossibly leathery hand would pull
a chit from its repository.
The going rate per punnet scrawled
in strawberry mulch above it: 60p.

Joel Scarfe
Balloons

The messages have been attached to the balloons,
helium-filled and ready to go. It's the summer
that the woman who would never burn
would burn in the sun, and after coming to the conclusion
that it must have had something to do
with the fallout, and that the Chernobyl sun's wick
had been turned up a notch, she would go
back out beneath its heat, as if enlisted
in some laborious war of attrition.

So here we stand, in a playground blasted clean
of any quaint innocence, releasing our balloons
into its teeming air. Watching open-mouthed
as their pale shadows are carried across the land.

Joel Scarfe
Disasters of War

Let the children sleep. They will not understand
the disasters of war. Barely anybody here
understands
the disasters of war, and so the kettle goes on
and a list of minor chores begin to form
in the mind. When we try to move around we struggle.
What we have learned about the disasters of war
is a formidable bag of stones
we must endeavour to pull behind ourselves
wherever we go. We long for the dumb intimacy
of childhood, of children's dreams,
where the only things to fall from the sky
are fairies and kisses and garish birds.
Let the children sleep. Don't let them wake
to the disasters of war
where nothing, not even the poem
can find the right words.

Mahvash Shafiei
This winter is a grave

1.
This winter is a grave,
Whose dead go to the morgues,
With pressed suits,
And in a land, at the end of this same afternoon,
They rise dead.

2.
We pass over each other corpses,
Like co-directional clouds,
We rain
On the inconclusive days.
There was no hand to be used in being found,
There was no eye to be used in remaining.
Someone within us is trying desperately to remain alive.

3.
Man was nothing more than a patch on the earth
We
Pieces fallen
Into bedrooms
Toilet
Kitchen.
Formal dresses
Televisions
Entangled
Regardless of how far we ascend, we did not get out of the earth
How far we jumped down, we did not fall from the bottom of anything
We watched and the play began with the plait of a woman's braid
Later on, we realized that we had been one side of the play.

Sue Skyrme and Chris Morley
Get On Yer Bike

Would you like to ride, fast and free under starry skies above
Get on yer bike, yer bike;

You can fly thro' the wide open country that you love
Get on yer bike, yer bike;

You can be by yourself in the evening breeze
Hear the distant murmur of the lorries wheels
And with any luck you won't get stung by bees
Get on yer bike.

Just hop on quick, you can straddle your gel saddle
underneath the Leicester skies, the Leicester skies;

And on your bike you can pedal past the traffic jams on
all those busy roads, those busy roads;

And when the price of petrol makes the car drivers bitter
Switch on your computer and then tweet on Twitter
That bikes are cheaper, cleaner and they keep you fitter

Get on yer...

Get on yer...

Get on yer bike.

Doo-wah.

Sam Smith
Give a slave a rod

'Give a slave a rod
and he'll beat his master'
                              - Old English proverb

The dutiful son of the estate owner
dutifully makes the annual inventory

which again includes the hectares of land owned
what loaned and leased, state of
the buildings, repairs required, amounts of
cotton / sugar / palm oil / latex produced;
what livestock, adult slaves
and their progeny
fit for sale.

(Given that latter listing what comes to this egalitarian mind are smudged
matchbox diagrams of slave berths, deck upon deck, and bills of lading
that tell of numbers lost in transit.)

To be fair the estate son did have resentments
- against expectations laid upon him,
to make a good marriage,
uphold the family name...
Respectability and all its confinements.

Jack So
Skating Through the Apocalypse

Mist transforms roads you thought you knew
like the brake at your heel. I stand where trees
in three directions swallow themselves in dead-end, then
fly. Headfirst into spun webs of rain choked aloft before
they can fall. And if I sing into the mist, will my answer
come from- or from within?

I swing my orbit past every other sphere making tracks,
hoping just once we meet. If the mist flares to
life between the corners of our eyes, might you be the
voice who sings back? If my coat billows a siren's deathbed
lament, will you sing back? If arms stretch the embrace of
a brass slide, will you sing back?
If my wheels skid on air and I
drop like a thief from the gallows, will you
sing?

A P Staunton
Brighton 84

Working in blood red Doc Martens,
Laying bricks in a Crombie coat,
Hair shaved to the bone, blue headed,
Called the English Channel "his moat".
"Keep an eye on the bird-lime, son,
We don't wanna work through our break."
Down the ladder, I would climb,
Two by two, the rungs I'd take,
To make his cuppa Rosy Lee,
With a spoonful of "Alan Sugar",
And a splosh of Acker Bilk,
Full fat, not that green-top bugger".
We gazed across the peeling piers,
On baccy tins we rolled our fags,
Sat on scaffold digestives dunking
Watching billowing Union flags.
"Makes ya proud don't it Paddy,
To live and work in the Promised Land…"
I bit my tongue and stared intently
At a hotel they called The Grand.

A P Staunton
Picture This

This is a man, who in Nineteen Sixty Three,
From County Louth, was forced to flee.
With a pregnant girl, they were not wed,
Priests outraged, riot acts read.
They shipped up in the South End, Liverpool Eight,
For the Africans and Chinese, more Irish mates.
This is a man, who stood like an animal in a pen,
To get a day's work at Gladstone Dock Ten.
If he kicked up a fuss at the graft and the pay
He wouldn't be picked for a shift the next day,
So, he took it on the chin and acted dumb,
To pay the rent on a two roomed slum.
This is a man, who worked his way up,
With friendship, loyalty, the occasional head butt.
This is a man who left life on the longshore,
For faraway ports in South America and Singapore.
This is a man who's hair started to bleach,
After laying two days drunk, on Waikiki Beach.
This is a man who came home to organise,
After learning the man who stands alone, is the man who dies.
This is a man, who challenged the bosses,
At Cunard, Cammel Lairds, John Wests, John Ross's.
Strikes were called and everyone was out,
No scabs, no fence sitters, this Union had clout.
They scrapped the Cages, for decent working practices,
A hundred years too late, a fucking fact that is.
This is a man who in Toxteth Eighty One,
Said "Son, put down that petrol bomb,
The police are too powerful, Thatcher's personal guard,
Corrupt, from the Bobby on the beat, right up to Scotland Yard."
This is a man, who waved me farewell,
As the industry died and the Union fell.
I roamed far and wide, as I'd been shown how,
To make a living, by the sweat of my brow.
With the swing of a pick and a well-heeled spade,
Foundations, for the rest of my life were laid.

This is a man, who lived by his own scripture,
And taught me, always, to see the bigger picture.

Tom Stockley
Hummus on Matzo

in between weak coffee
and hummus on matzo
Aunt Barbara tells me
about a town in Ukraine
called Chernigov
where a theatre takes the place
of the old synagogue
and laughter fills the space
that fear once knew so well.
no records remain
of my family
who once called those streets home.
she hands me a copy
of Uncle Joe's birthday speech;
i drink his memories, type-written
and taste words that, although new,
are literally *familiar.*
Cha - che - witz
she teaches me the syllables
of a name we are no longer known by
and tells me that this was only changed
when officials at Liverpool docks
told her uncles that their Jewish name
was too hard to pronounce.
the same uncles that,
only able to afford one passport
between them,
had to take it in turns to cross to their new life
hiding beneath the boardwalks and bows,
every hour getting further
from the bloodshed of their home.
if you look closely, you can still see
the cold streets of Chernigov
on my aunt's powdered cheeks
even though her mother only ever knew
the busy pavements

and flowing tichels
of girls in the East End.
she says when they were younger
they'd ask her mum to speak yiddish to them
but she would giggle,
the words already foreign
in the passing of one generation.

Tom Stockley
A Double Blessing

We are many parts, fractured.
We have always been here, scattered on the winds of every century.
We are pomegranate seeds in candlelight
and honey drops on plastic tablecloth.
We are lipstick traces and mascara smears on cheekbones,
unfinished in our form.
We hold moments of joy behind closed doors
and sadness in the streets.
We howl endlessly
and we are lost,
but never far from being found.
We are sages,
with wine and life upon our mouths
our ways are blessed and blameless.
We are new moons,
finding dreams in every month
and we are free children,
breaking from our chains.
We are infinite,
a doubling blessing on your homes.

Trefor Stockwell
Welcome to This Sceptred Isle

Torture, rape, fear, famine, war, persecution, or just a yearning for a better
life.
Whatever drives you to turn your back on all you know and love:
Your home, your friends, your way of life, your everything.
However great your despair there exists a beacon of hope:
A place of dreams, of freedom, a welcoming shore, that has embraced
many before:
Jew, Gentile, Muslim, Hindu, Sikh, received, succoured, assimilated and
then succeeded, even to the corridors of power.

Welcome to this Sceptred Isle.

That such a haven, such a paradise on earth, exists is hard to believe, but it
gives hope, drives you on.
Until one day you gather what few possessions you can carry, and set out
on a trip, so perilous, that we at home, cosy in our warm beds, can
barely conceive.
You cross seas, ford rivers, climb mountains, sustained only by your own
strength, courage, the all too rare kindness of strangers and your
dreams of salvation in a promised land.

Welcome to this Sceptred Isle.

Daily you face unimaginable dangers: friends die, are robbed, raped,
humiliated until one day you arrive at the last shore.
And gaze over that final seemingly narrow stretch of water.
God has been good, saved you from the many trials and tribulations,
surely, he will not desert you now, help you over this ultimate hurdle
and bring you safe home.

Parting with the last of your meagre wealth
You climb aboard the small craft
It seems so small, so fragile, so overcrowded, so inadequate to the task and
the journey too terrifying
But, with a final prayer to Allah, you set off anyway
It is cold, dark and the sea immense, oily-black and menacing

Frightening Leviathans loom, sightless and threatening to swamp your
   hopes
But somehow miss and sail on oblivious.
Some men bail frantically, some sink deeper in thought, women clutch
   their children protectively to their breasts while other silently pray.

Then it is over, you wade through the shallows
Emerge onto the steep shingle, fall to your knees, and kiss the pebbles of
   this long-imagined sanctuary.
They are cold, unyielding, salty and wonderful to taste.

Welcome to this Sceptred Isle.

The search-lights are frightening, the uniformed, unsmiling figures more
   so.
Orders are shouted, you are herded, given sweet tea and stand waiting to
   be 'processed'
What papers you have are taken, suspiciously scrutinised, stamped and
   filed until you stand uncertain before a desk.
The official does not return your smile before speaking:
"Sorry, dear migrants, it is such a shame
But you've become pawns in a political game.
Wrong creed, wrong colour, wrong race, wrong hue.
So, it's goodbye from us, and farewell to you.
Welcome to Britain, but your stay here is through
And your nightmare continues
Tomorrow
At Gatwick
Runway Two."

Welcome to this Sceptred Isle

George Symonds
A Breath of Bureaucracy

My grandma was a refugee
a Jew from Germany
She made it out, all on her own
with just her violin

Her family, they couldn't flee
because they didn't please
the ever strict bureaucracy
that noosed the refugees

She never saw them ever again
her mother, sister, nephew too

My grandma was a refugee
her maiden name, Israel

She said of those who gassed her loves,
"Bureaucracy kills"

George Symonds
British Beef

They say the meat we sell is honest,
One hundred per cent.
Implied in that, presumably,
That foreign beef misleads.
Maybe at the slaughterhouse,
We Brits make livestock confess,
Allegiance to Crown and Country,
Before stungun or knife brings death.

Sylvia Telfer
"That's Where the Black Men Are"

Way-back-when Black man, in cold and dank, did you recall
the scents of Africa—red soil of Senegambia and Windward Coast,
sensation of maize slithering through your fingers, that akin
plant with roots easily torn from loam, rumble of African
thunderstorm, haunting call of fish-eagle *weee-ah, hyo-hyo,*
cicada beetles noisy as a chainsaw? Or were you second-generation,
cut off from sensory memories? Either way, in some corner of your soul,
you might have grown peanuts on dunes and between them sorghum:
something sprouting from stories of ancestors. Far from ochre of Africa,
zilch for you in grey of Scotland's Leith docks but toil, hunger, fear,
boredom, and did you ever hear the white mothers shouting to kids,
"Never go down to the dockyards.
That's where the Black men are" and cry?
Ever wish to be a bird, so you could fly to sanctuary, reach
a known tree in which to nest?
In a photo, you're seen in 1910, wing-clipped, desolate, treeless,
free but abused. Sometimes curse your black skin?
But colour's only a concept, brother, devised by greed and slavery
and not just Black folks. Once, in Barbados, toiled white fishermen,
Irish slaves destined for scorched skin that rechristened them 'Redlegs'.
Their destitute offspring ever think of winter 1636 in which darkness
a ship slips out of Kinsale Harbour, of a sighing aspen when
patting a breadfruit tree, of a jackdaw's hard *tchack*
when catching on wind a purple-throated carib's sharp *chewp*?
But survival's key, the past must wait for safety.
So white, black, yellow, brown, red skin it's all
smoke and mirrors and the poor don't leave records:
stuff gets lost, history's written to thieves' tunes
Now, hyphenation's rife to stir the 'colour problem' pot
—*African-American, Anglo-Indian,* ad nauseum
and today learned bias in seeing an 'illegal immigrant'
on 'our streets' as a dark-skinned man passes by us.
History surrounds even in small stuff: chic scarf's from sweatshops
of China, Bangladesh, Nicaragua, Honduras, Viet Nam.
A tilted bag of sugar's plantations spilling into a bowl.
A bloke puffing on street's someone's sweat clouding air.

162

Tobacco, sugar, Black and poor white folk—merchandise.

A bell pepper can be orange, yellow, purple, brown,
black, ivory, green or red, but it's still a bell pepper.

"Where the Black men are" are words mothers in that era in Leith said to their kids. I wrote this poem years ago, and cannot find my original source but I have found a more recent source containing the same information in the comments section below the article, "Scotland and Slavery" (*Black History Month Magazine*, 19 August 2015 https://www.blackhistorymonth.org.uk/article/section/history-of-slavery/scotland-and-slavery/, accessed on 3 April 2023) where, on 17 December 2016, Viv Yeki wrote: 'My grandmother told stories to me as a child. She lived up the way from the Edinburgh dockyards where black Africans worked on ship building. The country was impoverished and it's economy relied on ship building. This was around 1910. Her mother put the fear of death in them never to go down to the dock yards. That's where the black men were.'

Critiques of the immigrant generation concept (Line 6) and the term 'illegal immigrant' (Line 31): Today, no legal or broadly accepted definition of 'irregular migrant' exists in UK, in which group are refused asylum seekers. The Black dock worker in the poem in 1910 would have been completely 'out on a limb'; certainly no media coverage to highlight his predicament, and very few groups working on his behalf.

History has proved promises by UK Government untrustworthy in terms of granting citizenship, the prime example being the 'Windrush Generation' who were let down because necessary legal paperwork was not produced nor were they made aware problems could arise from lack of documentation for those born in the UK to parents who are irregular migrants (who some 'Windrush Generation' unjustly became) means no birthright citizenship. Worse is it takes years for policy changes to go through the system, and changes are normally introduced only for newly arriving people.

Today, no legal or broadly accepted definition of a 'migrant' exists in UK law. The term 'migrant' in public discourse is loose. Sad is foreign low-skilled workers (like the Black docker in the poem who was probably no more than a slave) find it harder to gain legal status than students and high-skilled workers.

Ignorance in public understanding is in part due to false information put out by UK Government. For example, the United Nations says Rwanda is not a safe third country for the transfer of asylum seekers and the UNHCR say to proceed would breach the Refugee Convention, but Priti Patel told Parliament: 'Rwanda is a safe and secure country with respect for the rule of law', a claim the current Home Secretary, Suella Braverman incessantly repeats despite evidence to the contrary. Again, this highlights falsification and lack of compassion for potential Rwanda flight migrants who include victims of torture and human trafficking. The UK-Rwanda Deal is obviously a burden-shifting arrangement of the UK Government.

Very little has changed from the days of the Black docker in the poem, apart from rules and regulations on immigration, etc. having become more complicated (maybe deliberately so). Imperative new laws that are empathetic and not conflicting with each other need to be introduced. Every human being deserves compassion and a safe country regardless of whether or not it is their country of origin. The world is often referred to as "the global village" but that is not true for some.

Pam Thompson
Write This Down
Greenwich, December

What I believe in
is a star, hanging in the ship's rigging,
at 8am, frost on the grass in the park.
an orange sky, one or two people jogging,

the city, how it looks across the water
turning into its gleam, in its warm heart,
hidden under that gilt, that the green laser
arcs over plenty, not over poverty,

and the wren that flies in one door,
out of another on St Stephen's Day,
drops a feather, for luck,
in the lamplight in the hall,

and that ditching an umbrella
that turns inside out in a gale,
is the best thing, lets me press my body
into the wind, my face into the hail.

And what we take for love, at night,
like coal, burns steady and slow.
One of these natural resources (like bread,
water, milk) we take for granted, until it goes.

Pam Thompson
For Those On Beaumont Ward

For the woman with tattoos on her face and neck
who sits in the same place on the settee every day looking scared,
and for the young man who talks about his baby son,
and let's hear it for the woman in her dressing gown
whose hair's grey now but who used to dye it every colour,
and for the nurse who never keeps anyone stranded
in the middle of the floor, for those who lock and unlock doors.

Let's hear it for the young man who chats to everyone, shares
his baccy, even when he tells his mum and dad he's got no thoughts.
And for those who remember his birthday, sign his card, buy a cake,
though he's having the worst day, and for the young woman
who's loaded down with clothes because she's about to be discharged,

for those who give her a hug, say they'll miss her but don't
want to see her back, those who queue for medication,
or tense for an injection, for the noisy, for the mute.
For those waiting by the doors to be let out, for those who stay in bed,
for the man whose mother, father, sisters visit every day.
For those who never get a visit.

Let's hear it for all those who work here, wake up, sleep here.
For the visitors. Those who'll lose their beds if they go home on leave.
On this ward, and all the wards next to it.
                                        Let's hear it.

Beaumont Ward is in the Bradgate Mental Health Unit, Glenfield Hospital, Leicester.

Lauren Tormey
Permanently unsettled

I got my Indefinite Leave to Remain
That means no more questions, right?
I don't have to keep justifying why I should get to live here, right?
That's what I naively believed
Until the day I learned my new reality
That the UK border is an eternal visa application form
I just wanted to go home
But then the border agent asked me:
"How did you qualify for settlement?"
Excuse me?
Why do you need to know that?
My residency card doesn't even say that
Stop asking questions you don't need to know
Stop asking me questions full stop.

You gave me Indefinite Leave to Remain
The time for quizzing me is over
But I guess I can't refuse answering
I guess you always want me to feel at risk
You want to keep me in fear of losing my right to live here
You want to make sure immigrants know we're never welcome in the UK
That we never get to own our right to be here
You want to forever remind me I only get to live here because I once had a
    sponsor
Forever a guest
Forever owned

Indefinite Leave to Remain doesn't mean what I thought it would
I once equated it with permanency
But now I know
Only one thing is permanent with settlement in the UK:
Feeling permanently unsettled

Deborah Tyler-Bennett
Homage to a Migrant
North Bersted Man*

How come you rest here, soldier of Gaul,
rook's flight from Chichester, from tesserae
of Fishbourne? Kennings chant sky-
skeletons, hillside burials feast-halls for
flesh-peckers. Celts glimpsing Morrigans,
shawls spread on bones.

Did they honour with scabbard, dagger,
shield? Death's outer shores prove
cumbersome. Missing owl flight, clash
of brown hare, snow weighed branch,
missing sun on my face, salting this tongue.

Talisman-trove for 'warriors of standing',
maybe Chief of Bellovaci,
helmet's fretwork liver spotted.
Soldier of Gaul. Chariot
staves gone to earth,
ash-grave … cherry-splinter.

Shards proclaim: all *die migrants,*
sure as ice melt; sockets claggy with foreign soil
I lie here, your discovery; know last breath sped
crow sure, jet rag blown miles off course, hopped
to halt beneath childhood's sacred sky.

---

*North Bersted Man a 'mystery warrior' was exhibited at The Novium, Chichester in 2020. No one
knows how a Gallic warrior came to be buried near Chichester.

Morrigans - Celtic Crow Women/ Kennings – Old English and Norse riddling poetic forms.

Elizabeth Uter
Stitch Up

Dear UK,
I've seen a pattern emerge, a knitted, knotted stitch
I've had to unpick alongside the unpacked, battered
baggage of my Windrush Ma and Pa — their Caribbean dreams

like crates once full of sun-kissed oranges, once lining up
with hope and light streaming through the slats — checking in with
their serenity — their sovereign, mental map opened up to

a grey day, British reality of *No Blacks, No Irish, No Dogs* — I have
had to cut my eye on history — Afro-stick my spitting hair, cream
the darkened pigment of my skin to shine brighter than the

burgundy, golden oldie passport. Brush up my old girl accent,
be a sport — today, perceive deeply the meaning of — first generation
— *living* in *a hostile environment* — cheers mate —*Teresa* may say:

It was just the day's policy — embroider the tale — untangle
the sordid facts. It's just that these aged peepers have seen the hate
protests — the BNP, the UKIP skip a heartbeat — thugs leaving behind

bleeding chunks from black-born heads and brown.
Heard the ocean between sounding the name *Reform Party*
— watched the waves embracing, cosying up, tea-partying

with strange bedfellows both across the pond, and, in Engalund
— it has come to this — born and bred yet not accepted here
nor even where the parents hail from — called with no irony,

no twist of lip — *English Gal in* their *back home,* JA, Mobay.
My face is unravelling, dropping a stitch. Each second
caught within a broken net that catches some whilst

others slip. You call me many things — it's not as if sticks
and stones don't have a choice of voice. *Identity.* I'm loosing
the thread of the conversation — the warp and weft of red mist,

arguing words don't matter — *white s'alright, browns hang
around and black that's that* and always gaslit by the term
Afro-Caribbean. I mean, seriously, I'm no by-blow hairdo.

In this green, unpleasant land, black is seen as deviant,
not the norm, mud under foot but only in relation to the pure,
white shores and if it's all the same to you I'm not BAME either.

Better call me individual of African Origin as *Descent* implies
a fall, and *would you Adam and Eve it* — we all know the peg
that one hangs on — lessons learnt —- stitched up by the *othered* song,

conditioned to not belong — ha — wiser now — I'm cock-a-hoop, hooking the loop,
connecting me with Africa's rich, life fabric, no more drifting strands to make my whole
break apart — I suppose, now, I'm too clever by half to be needled by you, UK.

Elizabeth Uter
Parliament Litter

The war dogs are barking in the back benches of Westminster
 — the front ones used as loungers for ill-bred scroungers with
double-barrel names — inconceivable, unbelievable these peevish

specimens shivering with tails between their legs get to say how
we should live our lives: the whole howling pack of them, stomachs
on the growl for the next tea break — fine dining all day long,

whilst nurses, teachers, children live on the breadline begging for
a mug, drooping in myriad Soup Kitchens — *free food* has a price
but is given pride of place — when charity has to bridge the disparity gap

in wealth, health in a crumbling society — it's not a nice taste: to have wages
so low they break you, make you strike — whilst those overdogs in their ivory
lairs power the world with vice — watching us mice scurry in a hurry to dine

on dying. We are crying, trying to apply a living in a loveless hell.
These mongrels, curs, bitches stitch us up, spurning opportunities to do the decent,
altruistic thing for community's sake. They act with impunity: think Paradise Papers

 — think off-shore for more money than they can wrap their fetid, sweated bodies in.
They never learn, gurning to cameras, social media — *sound bites* make them seem
alright. Propaganda, slogans — they've become feudal shoguns as the country burns:

Brexit, pandemic, demonic, monarchic mischief of a little prince airing his *#MeToo*
dirties on the line when *Mummy* should be obeyed — we watch him stumble into slime.
Our Queen gives us cake — no one blushing with shame over a Platinum Jubilee game

 — where so much money wasted on pomp and ceremony — could've been used
on essentials — lasting so many days in a *cost of living crisis*. In this uncommon era:
rogues prorogue and the Commons summons dumb us to death, the tedium of being

where *canines dream* of chasing broken birds, us — hunting — sensing the blood of others.
All the *mutts* are present, correct — all wanting to be Top Dog because pups must bow,
roll-over, show their tummy, neck. Bellies gorged with wine — this *animal farm* is turning

into swine — stomachs full as foie gras about to burst — good government servants
so rare they are like priceless delicacies, barely glimpsed within a lifetime.
The hounds are battling for their lives, their right to feather-line fat pockets

already busting at the seams. Taking second homes, second jobs without a blink
 — one considers it his right to buy a tree house for his child — the price of a small home
the everyday man dreams of owning, imagine 150,000 sterling of our hard earned cash

nearly going, going gone on a littlun? A pad for a two year old — then imagine
wall to wall inelegance spread about that *Number 10* tat, as gaudy as a bawdy house.
Look, look, read like a book, really look at parliament: *a pox on both your houses.*

A pretence of meritocracy but as backwards as a shady kakistocracy.
Nepotism, cronyism, authoritarianism — every schism, ism is alive,
thriving in those clutching, chubby, grubby greedy, seedy paws.

Elizabeth Uter
The Condition

F**k that for a laugh, they are having a giraffe. Universal Credit,
government being Nanny handing over selective sweets that aren't
a treat but the only means that many can live off now the economy's

tanked. Thanks. Totally banged to rights as Boris like Nero, dithers, twitters,
watches UK burn. F**k their largesse that comes at a price, gouge out
the grey men's eyes —- put out the far right light — their sick f**k reluctance

to give a helping hand with school dinners outside school times, in the middle
of a pandemic. It's only common decency, kindness. Imagine that's your kid,
belly heavy with the going without food? Benevolent despots in their rancid,

smiling decadence. Lucky you, who gets to choose to trip out to a castle and
refuse to socially distance, dragging along an ailing wife. We see you selfishly
carry privilege on your crooked back. You know who you are, what you did

— in a castle gardened from *our Covid fugue* — *whilst* in a trance, we danced
on the tips of pins, desperate to get a spark of light, make life right — a gleam
of metal warmth — the closest we could get to coin — lest we forget, you want

to rid us of our pounds and pence. Crypto. Our Gov's become a Stasi agent
monitoring us by swipe of card and more. Hard to forget the freedom days
that weren't real freedom anyway. No true democracy but one throttled, leashed in

at the neck, brought to heel by brave, new conditioning — we didn't even know
we'd had a bad batch of '*Big-Brothering.*' Soma or Victory Gin, love? Take your
pick. But here's the thing, there's this dance in our brain — the exchange of unseen

ideas that pop up, bubble in our head each second and flow into the creative juice
of rugged individualism. We are the weed peeping through the pavement's cracks
on a wet British morning. We are the wildling rose that finds a place to waft

her scent under the ole school boy's nose. We are free to roam in our minds.
Recapture the perfect day of a week ago, ten months past, even twenty years
when a Diamond Jubilee was scratching the surface of our delirium — and it's all

in the mind. We are all mind. We are all-seeing, should be believing, conjuring up
the life we wish … only visualise. Instead, we are clickbait kittens, cats behaving badly,
dogs being the bollocks, or whatever they do, deep down — but we are also raindrops

drifting from forehead to chin. We are nature — nurtured by it. We are the natural
environment, not rules and regulations, not straitjackets that make folk stiff mad.
All it takes is the unsuspecting smile on an anonymous face as we turn and catch

a stranger by surprise —— heavenly union, communion, they smile back, we nod,
we do not distance as and when we're told — conditioned to do — f**k that, we make
a human connection, reaching towards each other as we humans are supposed to do.

Michael Walling
Who are we now to welcome you?

Who are we now to welcome you?
After the desecration of the sacred places
After the unearthing of the children's bodies
After the cynical breakage of the binding treaties
Who are we now to welcome you?

After the genocide against the buffalo
After the coming of the measles and the smallpox
After the systematic reduction of reservation land
After the demonising of spirituality, culture and language
After the banning of institutional generosity
Who are we now to welcome you?

After the forced removal of children
After the trauma of abuse
After the disappearances of so many women
After the rape of the land
After the suppression of hunting and fishing
Who are we now to welcome you?

After the imposition of alien governance
After the wrangling over blood quantum and status
After the unfettered arrogance of missionaries and teachers
After the propagation of a multicultural myth
After the tacit acceptance of sexual abuse
Who are we now to welcome you?

Michael Walling
On this land also

On this land also
there once were women
who were wise
in the ways of the waters

herb lore
plant lore
the paths of healing
across the plains of Mercia.

In time
they came to be known as
witches
and some were burned - like trees - to ashes

And yet they are not gone
their dust is in this land
that was their mother
as they were mothers
daughters
sisters

Here beneath our feet
under the pavements and the parks
wound around the roots of the Douglas Fir
shoring the foundations of the squat Empress's pedestal
hidden but not gone from the world armaments hub
The Gun Quarter
Jewellery Quarter
Fort Dunlop
Hippodrome
Bullring

they are with us
in the land.

They whisper
They murmur

"Let us emerge beside you
into a time of healing
with ceremony, that offers change and hope,
with poetry
with dance."

Matthew James Wiegel
I found my body yesterday for the first time again

I found my body yesterday for the first time again,
when the ice melted just a little, and I almost slipped.
I caught myself,
and I held myself in a way that only my body could.

the steps I took were reconsidered
and only considered viable in relation to the water
and the shape the water took beneath my foot.
and every step was a new shape
every shape a new step

and the melting of me,
which would one day come as no surprise
would be a new body in this place
and nowhere else.

so to find yourself, in the shape of the places you have been is a
great honor
of the kind the spruce trees know,
with their roots stretching out for the ground their grandmothers grew in, and
knowing just how far the wind can carry you
while you are still forever home

in this body

where the earth is always patient for you
showing you the memory of grass
in the foot tickle
the funnel web
the breath of last year's seeds
and the welcoming magpie chatter

listen
that feeling of the earth beneath you
is the echo of the willows bouncing against each other like
the plucked strings of a symphony
and the wind through the hairs of your body

Michele Witthaus
One Day Soon

Take heart, my dear.
Once again you will
take for granted
going for coffee with friends
and conversing with strangers,
picking up the scarf
dropped by the woman
at the next-door table
and passing it back
with a smile.

Once again you will
smile at market traders
and hold the post office door
for other souls
who have drifted far from home.
You will send letters
padded with small treats
that tell those you left behind
that you are all right
so they can stay strong.

Once again you will
merge with the crowd
in the place
where you also live
and let the people carry you
in their midst,
trusting in your belonging
as much as theirs.
Take heart, my dear.
You're almost there.

Michele Witthaus
Between Lives

I tried
    so hard
        not to become
           one of those
              who mourn
                  the heartbeat
                    of home.
                        And yet
                            when I
                      remember
                      all that I left
                  I fall under a spell
              of stunned sadness
           because I went
      not lightly but
    too soon
  and too late
to return.

Gregory Woods
Godless Practices

You take control of our land
and you take control of our people.

You release a swarm of priests
to call us all ungodly
and you institute a law
to stamp out godless practices,
the signs of our barbarity.

You release a swarm of judges
in sweltering gowns and wigs,
too hot for the tropics.

Many decades pass.
You grant us independence
in our own land,
but leave your laws in place
and our infected priests and judges.

You decide to allow
those same godless practices
in your own land
and change your view of them
as many decades pass.

Our judges swelter on
in their gowns and wigs,
too hot for the tropics,
too hot for mercy or restraint.

You even start to think
our sticking to your law
a sign of our barbarity.
Your priests debate our godlessness.

Threatened by your law

in our own land,
some of us flee our land
for yours,
seeking out your godliness
in yours.

And when we reach your land,
seeking refuge from your law

—the law you imposed on us
but from which you released
your own people—

when we seek asylum, do you grant it?

Nina Worthington
Truth Unseen

They tell me that my dreams have changed, but whose dreams were they
    anyway?
The dream of a country that believes we must conform, be 'normal', to be
    okay,
A dream where difference is feared and understood as loss,
Yet the truth unseen by many is having a child like mine is gain, more than
    cost.

In other families of two-point-four, pride is found in acceptance at a top
    university,
Yet, pride of families like mine is measured in small feats, slow and steady,
The independent shopping trip, new friendships, a slow-typed essay,
A meal eaten without support, or clothes chosen in a hurry.

What the world can't see is how this brings perceptions of great worth,
Assumed loss others think I must come to terms with, instead, is freedom
    from all I've ever learnt,
New understanding of daily struggles, so trials won't bring life crashing
    down,
An acceptance of others without the judging frown,
A capacity to think beyond the lies we're always sold,
That success is made in fast-paced living and lone pursuit of all that's gold.

There's dependence in my family, not weakness, but strength to let other
    people in,
A life sometimes unglamorous, but builds courage to really dream,
Of a society where success is understood as being truly me,
Not trying to fit in a box that was never meant to be.

So don't pity me, assuming loss, I'm freed from so-called normality
By living with experiences of disability that will be tasted by one in three,
So, when it's your turn don't be afraid or believe the lies they'll say,
That your freedom to really live will be taken away.
Instead embrace a world where value in uniqueness is revealed, explained,
Embrace a life of fullness, where difference is real gain.

Neelam Wright
White Mask

I gave compassion, confidence, drive
You received darkness, threat, aggression.
I sang with courage, conviction, honesty
But you preferred the melody of reserved chit-chat
The endless song of polished apologies.
I can walk on fire stones
But you gave me a path of broken glass.
I offered to dismantle walls with movement, volume, vibrancy
You built new walls with collective inertia and pastel visions.
You command I speak in your words, your tone, to your taste
But I cannot
You ask me to be your shield when it suits you and silent when it does not
I will not.
I will not.
You permit boldness if I remain subservient
A dog unleashed from its chains only when it suits the owner
I am not your wild animal to tame.
Accept me as I am or do not call yourself an ally
Decipher *my* way of being, as I have yours
So that I may speak with the powerful voice that my ancestors gave me.
Difference is my virtue, my energy source
Wearing your White mask
I suffocate.

Trevor Wright
Biscuit Tin Dreams

Welcome friend. We will do our best to make sure
that you and your family are able to settle and prosper.

But first, I must tell you of a dream many of us have,
a recurring, disturbing dream in which someone sings
what you think are your songs, paints what you think
are your pictures, solemnly presents you with your
very own fanfare and flag and Busby biscuit tin.

A well-turned-out man puts a long arm lightly across
your shoulder, uncurls a silken finger, points east as
he speaks softly of oncoming tsunamis, whispering
it's time, be vigilant, stiffen your spine in anticipation
or it will swamp every corpuscle of you and yours.

You look to the horizon and think that you can pick
out the tell-tale signs of a draining ocean but wake in
a cold sweat before the waters rise and whilst the well-
turned-out man is nowhere to be seen you can still
sense that warm reassuring arm across your shoulder.

Once showered and dressed, you realise that all
your pockets have been deftly picked clean. You
take to the biscuit tin for comfort, caress its sepia
sides. On opening, it's shorn of sustenance, just rust
and the stale whiff of someone else's nostalgia.

So, welcome, friend. What say you that we together, draw
out much finer blueprints for our children's dreams?

Duaa Zahida
Seeds of Hope

we feel   inside the fence
          where life is miserable

     on the other side
it's full of life and colour

     we have no place
          in our countries
   and we are not given a chance
       here

i sow seeds of hope
     in poisonous soil

i will pray

let's see if my prayer wins
     or if the poison will

Kathy Zwick
The Cartographer's Burden

Let's rethink outdated prejudices,
reduce the giant bloated Greenland blob.
Redraw the correct size of Africa,
so, aid agencies can do their proper job.

Applaud Arno Peters' elongated continents,
reject Mercator's meridian control.
Move on from old Eurocentric bias,
the Southern Hemisphere has paid its toll.

Replace outdated old chap Mercator's myth
drawn to the imperial navigator's need.
Reappraise colonisation and empire,
allow a newer truer map to succeed.

"Equal-Area" projections – a map justice dream.
Ahoy Rudyard: Maps are far more than they seem.

Gerardus Mercator (1512 – 1594)
Arno Peters (1916 – 2002)

Contributors

Sandra A. Agard is an honorary fellow of the Royal Society of Literature and has worked as a professional storyteller, writer, book doctor, cultural historian and literary consultant for over 40 years. She has performed and taught at venues and educational organisations across the UK and internationally. Agard has written numerous plays, poems and short stories and has had work published in a variety of collections and anthologies. Her books include *The Drum Maker and The Aziza* (2023), an African retelling of "The Elves and The Shoemaker"; *The Lion Keeper* (2022); *The Bristol Bus Boycott: A Fight for Racial Justice* (2022), and *Trailblazer: Harriet Tubman, A Journey to Freedom* (2019). She has also co-edited, with Laila Sumpton, *Where We Find Ourselves: Poems and Stories of Maps and Mapping* (2021).

Sarfraz Ahmed lives in the UK. His published books include poetry debut *Eighty-Four Pins: Poetry Collection* (June 2020) and *My Teacher's an Alien!* (November 2020). *Two Hearts: A Journey into Heartfelt Poetry* (February 2021) with Annette Tarpley and *Stab the Pomegranate: Collective Poetry* (August 2021). The second edition of *Eighty-Four Pins: Poetry Collection* was published in February 2022, followed by the global release of *The Gift of Poetry* (June 2022) specially dedicated to all his supporters. Sarfraz is an administrator at the large Passion of Poetry group on Facebook and has a following on Facebook and Instagram #sarfrazahmedpoet. In May 2021 he was recognised as a World Contributor Poet, recognised for his contribution to poetry by Administrators, Poetry and Literature World Vision. You can find him at open mic events, where he shares his poetry globally.

Jim Aitken's latest poetry collection is *Declarations of Love*, published by Culture Matters in 2022. He also works with Adult Education in Edinburgh, teaching a course called *Scotland in Union and Disunion*.

Malka al-Haddad is an Iraqi academic and poet. She has a Masters degree in Arabic Literature from Kufa University in Iraq. She is a graduate of the University of Leicester where she studied for a Master of Arts degree in the Politics of Conflict and Violence. Her debut poetry collection, *Birds Without Sky: Poems from Exile* (Harriman House Ltd, 2018) was longlisted for the Leicester Book of the Year award in 2018.

Judith Amanthis's short fiction and journalism have been published in Ghana, South Africa and the UK. Her novel *Dirt Clean* was shortlisted for the 2021 Paul Torday Memorial Prize. Her poetry has appeared in *Black Lives Matter*, *Untitled Writing*, *Write Across London*, *Sarasvati* and *Porridge*. She's a Londoner.

Marie Adrien Bitty is a writer and community builder, born in suburban Paris, France. She lives in Leicester, UK and, for more than a decade, has been building communities and delivering projects. In 2022, she joined a local poetry group, started performing and sharing her writing as well as collaborating on the translation and creation of theatre plays. Her main interests are in the use of creative writing and performing arts in supporting individuals in their recovery journey from the trauma of abuse and exploitation.

Anna Blasiak is a poet, writer, translator, and journalist. She has recently translated *According to Her* by Maciej Hen and also published a bilingual poetry and photography book (with Lisa Kalloo) *Kawiarnia przy St James's Wrena w porze lunchu / Café by Wren's St-James-in-the-Fields, Lunchtime*, as well as a book-length interview with a Holocaust survivor Lili. *Lili Stern-Pohlmann in conversation with Anna Blasiak*. She is one of the editors of Babiniec Literacki and the managing editor of the European Literature Network in the UK. annablasiak.com

Conor Blessing is a writer of weird fiction – all is possible in his stories. With inspirations ranging from Kelly Link, Carmen Maria Machado and all things animated, he writes about strange, yet loving, worlds slowly becoming infected by what others would call 'the norm.' He is also a recent graduate from Glasgow Caledonian University after studying International Fashion Business.

Paul Brookes is a shop assistant. His chapbooks include *A World Where* and *She Needs That Edge* (Nixes Mate Press, 2017, 2018), *The Spermbot Blues* (OPPRESS, 2017), *Please Take Change* (Cyberwit.net, 2018), and *As Folk Over Yonder* (Afterworld Books, 2019). He is a contributing writer of Literati Magazine and Editor of Wombwell Rainbow Interviews, book reviews and challenges. Had work broadcast on BBC Radio 3 The Verb and, videos of his Self Isolation sonnet sequence featured by Barnsley Museums and Hear My Voice Barnsley. He also does photography commissions. Most recent is a poetry collaboration with artworker Jane Cornwell: *Wonderland in Alice, plus other ways of seeing*, (JCStudio Press, 2021), and the sonnet collections: *As Folktaleteller* (ImpSpired, 2022), *These Random Acts of Wildness* (Glass Head Press, 2023), and *Othernesses* (JCStudio Press, 2023).

Martin Brown is Coventry born and bred, a retired health and social care worker and occasional poet, with a few published and prize-winning poems here and there, and two self-published books, *A Thousand Scary Cabbages* for children, and *Shake, Rattle and Custard* supposedly for adults.

Helen Buckingham lives in Wells, England. Collections include *water on the moon* (original plus press, 2010) and *sanguinella* (Red Moon Press, 2017), each of which was shortlisted for a Touchstone Award. She has work in a number of anthologies, including *Over Land, Over Sea* (Five Leaves Publications, 2015).

Philip Burton is a family man, born in Fife, raised in Thanet, and has been a hippie, a labourer, a professional student, and a Lancashire head teacher. In 2019, Philip Burton concurrently held four poetry competition First prizes: including the Jack Clemo, the Sandwich (Kent) Poet of the Year, and the Barn Owl Trust. He was winner of The East Riding Poetry competition 2021. His poetry publications include *The Raven's Diary* (joe publish, 1998), *Couples* (Clitheroe Books Press, 2008), *His Usual Theft* (Indigo Dreams Press 2017), *Gaia Warnings* (Palewell Press, 2021), and *The Life Dyslexic* (Palewell Press 2022).

Richard Byrt has written poems on diverse topics, and facilitates creative writing at SoundCafe Leicester, a charity for people who have many talents and abilities and have also experienced homelessness. Richard is actively involved in two poetry organisations in Leicester. His poems are published in anthologies, Glitterwolf LGBT magazine, and in his debut collection, *Devil's Bit*, edited by Sally Jack and published by De Montfort Press, Ltd.

Gareth Calway has published nine books of verse; a novel about teaching English in comprehensive schools and *Bound for Jamaica*, a children's book about the slave trade. He was series editor/author for Collins Education and now writes and performs in the combined arts duo Peacock's Tale with his wife Melanie. https://peacocks-tale.bandcamp.com

Yuan Changming hails with Allen Yuan from <u>poetrypacific.blogspot.ca</u>. Credits include 12 Pushcart nominations & 13 chapbooks (most recently *E.dening*) besides appearances in *Best of the Best Canadian Poetry* (2008-17), *BestNewPoemsOnline* & *Poetry Daily*, among others across 48 countries. Yuan served on the jury and was nominated for Canada's National Magazine Awards (poetry category).

Jo Cheadle is an artist and writer who wishes that they wrote more often than they currently do. She is a graduate of Lancaster University and now lives in Birmingham.

Marcus Christopherson is a Northern actor and poet.

David Clark is the London-born child of refugee parents and is currently on the editorial committee of Exiled Writers Ink, devoted to works by exiled and refugee writers. His poems have been published in *Second Generation Voices* (2009, 2014), *Contemporary Writers of Poland* (edited by Blaszak and Mickiewicz, 2015, 2020), *Voices Israel Poetry Anthology* (2019, 2021), *The Litterateur* (March 2021), *Mediterranean Poetry* (February 2022), *Southlight* (Spring 2022), *Ukraine in the work of international poets,* (Mickiewicz and Siemieńczyk, eds., 2022).

A C Clarke has published five full collections and six pamphlets, two of the latter, *Owersettin* and *Drochaid*, in collaboration with Maggie Rabatski and Sheila Templeton. Her fifth full collection, *A Troubling Woman* came out in 2017. She was one of four winners in the Cinnamon Press 2017 pamphlet competition with *War Baby*. She has been working on an extensive series of poems about Paul and Gala Éluard, later Gala Dalí, and the Surrealist circles in which they moved. The first set of these, *Wedding Grief*, was published as a pamphlet by Tapsalteerie last year (2021).

Julian Colton has had five collections of poetry published including *Everyman Street* (Smokestack Publishing), *Cold Light of Morning* (Cultured Llama) and *Two Che Guevaras* (Scottish Borders Council). He currently works Front-of-House at Sir Walter Scott's Courtroom Museum in Selkirk. For more info go to: <u>https://www.scottishpoetrylibrary.org.uk/poet/julian-colton</u>

Diana Coombes is a teaching assistant in a secondary school. She is a mother of two grown up children, one grandson, and granddaughter. Another addition to the family is her Rottweiler, German Shephard cross, Titan. Her domestic noir novel, *It Won't Happen Again*, was self-published in April 2021. Set in 2013, highlighting how domestic violence, especially at Christmas, can cause an environment of fear. Diana joined a playwright group, where she was part of a group of amateur writers. "The Kingswood Beast" premiered at The Corby Cube in 2022. In a contemporary style of play, viewed on VR360 headsets.

Mark Connors is a poet, novelist and creative writing facilitator from Leeds, UK. His debut poetry pamphlet, *Life is a Long Song* was published by OWF Press in 2015. His first full length collection, *Nothing is Meant to be Broken* was published by Stairwell Books in 2017. His second poetry collection, *Optics*, was published in 2019. His third collection, *After*, was published in 2021. He is currently at work on *MMXXII*, a hybrid book containing poetry, fiction, memoir and travel writing. Mark is a co-founder and a managing editor of YAFFLE PRESS.

Twenty years ago **Cardinal Cox** was the fifth Poet Laureate of Peterborough. Since then he has been poet-in-residence for a Victorian cemetery; a medieval church (from which came his collection *My Words Are Now Written*); and the Dracula Society. From that came his one-man show *High Stakes* (that was performed as far away as Helsinki and Dublin) and his second collection *Grave Goods* (released by Demain Publications). He has a small role with Peterborough Radical Book Fair that has an anti-racist, anti-sexist, anti-homophobia and positive agenda. He's untidy and easily distracted. Something, something, something.

Heaven Crawley is a researcher with the UN University Centre for Policy Research in New York but has worked at the universities of Swansea and Coventry, as well as the UK Home Office and a range of community and non-governmental organisations and think-tanks. Heaven's work focuses on the inequalities with which migration is often associated including those relating to race, gender and age, as well as the ways in which these inequalities intersect with nationality and place to shape migration experiences and outcomes. She has three children and four grandchildren and currently lives in Italy.

Robin Daglish is a retired builder of 74. He self-published his first pamphlet, *Rubies*, in 2002 to celebrate the birth of his granddaughter and his first full collection, *Weymouth Dawn*, in 2012. Published in many magazines and anthologies, currently living near Brighton, he is active in the local performance poetry scene as 'Brickybard.'

Emer Davis is a poet from Ireland. She has lived and worked in London, Abu Dhabi, Lesvos Island in Greece and India. Her poems have been published widely and she came second in the Trocaire Poetry Ireland competition with her poem Raqqa Bowl 2017. She published two poetry collections in India about her experiences there. More information can be found on her website Bunnacurrypoet.org and on her Bunnacurry Poet facebook page.

Craig Dobson has had poems published in Acumen, Agenda, Antiphon, Bandit Fiction, Butcher's Dog, CivicLeicester, Crannóg, The Dark Horse, The Frogmore Papers, Ink, Sweat and Tears, The Interpreter's House, Lighten Up Online, The Literary Hatchet, The London Magazine, Magma, Neon, New Welsh Review, The North, Orbis, Pennine Platform, Poetry Ireland Review, Poetry Salzburg Review, Prole, The Rialto, Stand, Southword, THINK and Under The Radar.

Kimia Etemadi is a writer, translator, interpreter and teacher from Manchester, England. She loves travelling, learning languages, and experiencing different cultures. She has lived in six countries and visited more than forty.

James Farson is a writer born, bred, and based in Peterborough. His passions include science fiction, rock music, and Arsenal Football Club. At university James won the Ian Gordon Prize for best dissertation for his work on James Joyce's Ulysses, and after graduating from Anglia Ruskin with an English Literature degree in 2013 he has continued to develop his interest in fiction and poetry. By day he works for a charity in Peterborough.

Max Terry Fishel. Born Liverpool to European Jewish parents. Lives London. Worked NHS, education. Now "retired". Plays Irish instrumental music in London sessions. Loves performing, and Dutch salt liquorice. Writes poems/songs/tunes. Does open mic spots with gusto.

Corinne Fowler is Professor of Colonialism and Heritage in Museum Studies at the University of Leicester. She directs a child-led history and writing project called Colonial Countryside: National Trust Houses Reinterpreted (2018-2022, Heritage Lottery and Arts Council). In 2020 she co-authored an audit of peer-reviewed research about National Trust properties' connections to empire. The report won the Museums and Heritage Special Recognition Award, 2022. Her most recent book is *Green Unpleasant Land: Creative Responses to Rural England's Colonial Connections* and her next book is *The Countryside: Ten Walks Through Colonial Britain* (Penguin Allen Lane: Spring 2023).

Paul Francis is a retired teacher, living in Much Wenlock. He is a versatile and prolific poet, active in the West Midlands poetry scene, who has won national prizes. His work includes the poetry collections, *Rescue from the Dark* (Fair Acre Press) and *Poems for Ukraine* (Liberty Books).

Marsha Glenn is trying to make Britain her home for the last ten years. She is a member of the creative writing group Write to Life at Freedom from Torture charity organisation.

Barrington Gordon is a published author. He has a poem in the anthology, *Poetry and Settled Status for All*. One of his short stories, "The Chair" was published in *Voice, Memory, Ashes: Lest We Forget*. Another of his stories, "Grandfather's Feet" was published in *Whispers in The Walls*, a Birmingham anthology endorsed by Bonnie Greer and Benjamin Zephaniah. BBC Radio 4 also featured this tale.

Roger Griffith is a writer, activist and social entrepreneur.

Originally from the Philippines, **Rosario Guimba-Stewart** came to England in 1995. Her first job in the UK was with the Refugee Council. In 2010, she joined the Lewisham Refugee and Migrant Network (LRMN) as their CEO. Her poetry is inspired by her experience as an immigrant and the people she meets.

Prabhu S. Guptara's poems have been published since the 1960s in magazines, in anthologies, and in two collections. In January 2017, Skylark Publications, UK, chose him as its Poet of the Month. He is included in Debrett's *People of Today*.

Monique Guz is working on a debut novel. Her work has been featured in *Poetry and Settled Status for All*, *The Other Side of Hope: Journeys in Refugee and Immigrant Literature*; Late Britain; and Placeholder Press. She was also a mentee on the 2020 National Centre for Writing Escalator scheme.

Kim Hackleman is a lover of peace, mother of boys, director, actor, producer and writer. Selected writing as follows: "I Too Am an Immigrant" in the anthology *Poetry and Settled Status for All*. "Weaving Coventry" commissioned by Coventry City Council and in granite relief in the water rills in Coventry city centre. "Birthday Gifts – A Visual Installation" commissioned by Coventry City of Culture Trust and the Royal Shakespeare Company for *Faith*. A collection of poems as part of *Our Wilder Family*, the longest drone show in the UK and one of the final events of Coventry UK City of Culture.

scott manley hadley (@Scott_Hadley) was 'Highly Commended' in the Forward Prizes for Poetry 2019. Publications include *Bad Boy Poet* (Open Pen, 2018), *My Father, From A Distance* (Selcouth Station Press, 2019) and *the pleasure of regret* (Broken Sleep Books, 2020). Scott, who has been diagnosed with Borderline Personality Disorder, blogs about mental health and literature at *TriumphoftheNow.com*

Nusrat M Haider works in the NHS as a trainee nursing associate. She has contributed to the following anthologies: *Leicester 2084 AD*, *Bollocks to Brexit*, *Wondering Minds*, *Black Lives Matter*, and *Poetry and Status Settled for All*. She has also won the Leicester Women's Poetry Prize in 2022. Nusrat enjoys reading fiction and likes to write in her free time.

M-L Chika Haijima is a mother of two children. Born in London, daughter of an Italian mother and Japanese father. Has a Masters in English Literature from the University of Warwick and currently works in Higher Education as Deputy Head of Student Experience. Writing has always been a key part of her life and she hopes to complete her book as well as a compilation of children's short stories, both of which focus on belonging, acceptance and diversity.

Patricia Headlam is a UK-based poet who loves to write about self-healing and anti-racism. She is a member of a local poetry group and has recently started reading her poems at public events.

Alanah Hill is a sociology PhD student at Lancaster University. Her research focuses predominantly on Lancaster and the Transatlantic Slave Trade, in particular examining the lives of the Satterthwaite family who were one of an array of Lancastrian families with significant involvements in the trade. Through various research projects surrounding Lancaster and slavery, Alanah found that poems were the most suitable method for portraying the emotions, stories and lives of enslaved people often omitted from popular discourses on the British Empire and colonialism.

Louisa Humphreys lives in Leicester and works as a dragonfly party coordinator.

Cathryn Iliffe is a retired Biology college tutor and research scientist, part time poet and archaeology student. Her family comes from Sapcote, Leicester, where they went from being impoverished non-voting stocking-knitters, to prosperous Victorians, to impoverished citizens in the Great Depression. She tries to spend as much time as possible in the wilds.

Nnamdi Christopher Iroaganachi is a poet and writer with an interest in culture, history and the world. He is an avid learner, fan of the United Kingdom and its language, the Queen's English.

Jade Jackson was born in East Africa, studied journalism and worked as a sports reporter. After members of her family were killed and her own life was threatened, Jade was forced to flee and arrived in the UK in 2001. Jade volunteers at the Refugee Council, published her first collection of poetry, *Moving A Country*, in 2013, and regularly recites her work in the UK.

athina k is in a permanent midlife crisis and writes poetry to battle the horror of everyday life in England.

Ziba Karbassi was born in Tabriz, north western Iran. She has been writing poems from an early age. Her first book in Persian was published in her early twenties. Since then, she has been published regularly, not only in her mother tongue but internationally. She was chairperson of the Iranian Writers Association (in exile) from 2002 to 2004, director of pen international relations (Iran, in exile), from 2019 to the beginning of 2021, and chair of Exiled Writers Ink in UK, from 2012 to 2014.

John F Keane lives in Manchester, in the UK. A software developer, he has published poems in a number of British anthologies and publications. These include *Prole* (2010), *Best of Manchester Poets Volume 3* (2013), the *Live from Worktown Anthology 5* (2018), the *Poetry from the Platform Anthology* (2021) and *The Bread and Roses Award Anthology* (2022). In addition, he has published poems in a number of international publications including Analog, the American speculative fiction magazine and Jubilat, literary journal of the University of Massachusetts. He also won Bolton Station's Community Partnership contest in 2020 and gained top honours in the 2021 Ekphrastic Poetry Contest sponsored by the Friendswood Public Library, Texas.

Yessica Klein is a Brazilian-born writer based in Berlin after stints in São Paulo, London, Liverpool, and Lisbon. Yessica got her MA in Creative Writing from Kingston University (UK) and her writing has been featured on 3:AM, SALT., The Moth, Magnum Photos, The Lighthouse Review, and more. She was also shortlisted for the 2021 Aesthetica Creative Writing Award and the 2017 Jane Martin Poetry Prize.

Phil Knight is a poet and political activist from Neath in South Wales. He has been published in Red Poets, Earth Love, Poetry Wales, Atlantic Review, Planet and other publications.

Jennifer Langer is founding director of Exiled Writers Ink. Her debut poetry collection is *The Search* (Victorina Press, 2021) and she is editor of five anthologies of exiled literature (Five Leaves Publications). She holds a doctorate in Cultural Memory from SOAS, University of London and is a SOAS Research Associate. She is the daughter of refugees from Nazi Germany.

Zahira P Latif is a former academic and a British Pakistani Muslim woman from a working-class background. She has had creative non-fiction pieces published in the British Literary Magazine, Porridge and the Wilderness House Literary Review, and is currently working on her first non-fiction book – a polemical critique of the implications of capitalism on our well-being. She lives with her family in Birmingham, England, United Kingdom. Twitter: @zplatif

Charles G Lauder, Jr, was born and raised in San Antonio, Texas. He lived briefly in London in 1987-8, and then fully immigrated here in 2000, where he currently lives with his family in South Leicestershire. He's published two pamphlets, *Bleeds* and *Camouflaged Beasts*, and his debut collection, *The Aesthetics of Breath*, was published in 2019 by V.Press.

E B Lipton is a poet and short story writer whose work has been published in the UK, India, and Israel. Prizewinner in the International Reuben Rose Competition 2020. Member of Exiled Writers Ink. She lives in London.

Rob Lowe continues to enjoy having his political and philosophical poems accepted for online and/or print publication, approximately one a month over the past five years. He is grateful for the commitment Editors make in providing these platforms, and hopes that the hard work of writing poetry makes a difference in the world.

Jacob Lund's poetry has been published in journals and anthologies across the UK and Europe. These include *The Use of English*, *N2*, *Openings*, *Bollocks to Brexit*, *Pro Saeculum* and *Banchetul*. He is a regular writer for the poetry magazine of The Open University, and has also published on Shakespeare, Donne and literary theory for The English and Media Centre and for NATE. Once a fiction reviewer for a national newspaper, he has for fifteen years taught English Literature, and currently works at Varndean College, Brighton.

Walid Marmal is a London VOICES Network Ambassador. An educator, journalist, editor, producer, broadcaster, and translator, he is also a strong human rights activist. His recent Beirut-based work was as a producer and broadcaster of two television programmes exploring religion, philosophy, and current political developments. He has previously served as a volunteer and activist in several US-based organisations, including the Boy Scouts of America, and the Michigan Chapter of Amnesty International. He also founded IMAN and co-founded IRSHAD, two organisations that promote dialogue and inclusion. Walid has a special interest in poetry (Arabic and English) and is currently editing his collection.

Fokkina McDonnell now lives in The Netherlands. She has three poetry collections (*Another life,* Oversteps Books Ltd, 2016; *Nothing serious, nothing dangerous,* Indigo Dreams Publishing Ltd, 2019; *Remembering/Disease,* Broken Sleep Books, 2022) and a pamphlet (*A Stolen Hour,* Grey Hen Press, 2020). Poems have been widely published and anthologized. Fokkina received a

Northern Writers' Award from New Writing North in 2020 for her third collection. Sheblogs on www.acaciapublications.co.uk where she also features a guest poet each month.

Nicollen Meek is a writer living in London with her two cats. Her previous work has been published in the anthology, *Bollocks to Brexit.*

Jenny Mitchell has won several poetry competitions including the Poetry Book Awards, and is a Forward Prize nominee. The best-selling debut *Her Lost Language* is One of 44 Poetry Books for 2019 (Poetry Wales). Her second collection, *Map of a Plantation,* is a set text at Manchester Metropolitan University, and her third collection *Resurrection of a Black Man* is a Poetry Net Book of the Month. Publisher: Indigo Dreams.
Twitter: @JennyMitchellGo

Born in Namibia, and living her teenage years in Belfast during the height of "the troubles", **Colleen Molloy** is sensitive to issues of racism, prejudice and the narrative of people who migrate, especially to find sanctuary. She is new to writing poetry, having joined Word! workshops after retirement from City of Sanctuary UK. Her poems are from her experience in hosting, supporting and listening to people seeking asylum, especially about their journeys and the cruel indifference of the UK Home Office.

Helen Moore is an award-winning British ecopoet and socially engaged artist with three collections, *Hedge Fund, and Other Living Margins* (2012), *ECOZOA* (2015), acclaimed as 'a milestone in the journey of ecopoetics', and *The Mother Country* (2019) exploring British colonial history. Helen offers an online mentoring programme, Wild Ways to Writing, which guides people on a creative writing journey into deeper Nature connection. Her work is supported by Arts Council England, and she has recently collaborated on a cross arts-science project responding to pollution in Poole Bay and its river-systems. www.helenmoorepoet.com

Hubert Moore's thirteenth full collections include *Owl Songs* (2021*), Country of Arrival* (summer 2022) and the latest, *Hello dear* which is now at the printers. All three of the latest collections are from Shoestring Press. Most of Hubert's collections have all contained poems which express his concern for refugees in the UK. Between 2000 and 2010 he was a writing mentor with Freedom from Torture and a visitor at Dover Immigration Detention Centre.

KE Morash is a playwright and poet from Nova Scotia, now living in the UK. Her writing has received prizes and been published in Gyroscope, Raceme, Spelt, Ink, Sweat & Tears, Songs of Love & Strength; Room; and Understorey; amongst others. She won first place in the Sentinel Literary Quarterly Prize, was twice shortlisted for the Live Canon International Poetry Prize and longlisted for the National Poetry Prize.

Chris Morley is a retired social worker and feminist who has sung with Red Leicester Choir since it began. She cares about the environment and social justice and enjoys campaigning through song as well as through her involvement with Quakers. She enjoys walking and birdwatching and being creative with words and fabric. Her values are shaped by her strong commitment to making a difference in the world through grass roots activism on environmental issues, nature conservation and human rights.

Loraine Masiya Mponela is a social justice campaigner living in England. She has a lovely son, and is the author of *I was not born a sad poet*, her book of poetry.

Gil Mualem-Doron is an award-winning transdisciplinary artist, photographer, curator and cultural activist. Based on his lived experience of displacement, he investigates liminal identities and places, transgressive spaces, decolonial practices and transcultural aesthetics. Much of his work is created through collaborative and participatory practices that lead to the creation of social and physical spaces that transcend everyday life. Having a PhD in Architecture and a particular interest in urban histories, much of his work is site-specific and interactive. His socially engaged photographic work has been a direct negation of his military service as an air photographer and a search for alternative modes of representation. With a deep involvement in social and political movements, some of his works are transgressive and not easy to digest. More about Gil Mualem-Doron's work can be found at www.gmdart.com or on Instagram Gil_Mualem_Doron

Ambrose Musiyiwa coordinates Journeys in Translation, an international, volunteer-driven project that is translating poems from *Over Land, Over Sea: Poems for those seeking refuge* (Five Leaves Publications, 2015) into other languages. Books he has edited include *Poetry and Settled Status for All: An Anthology* (2022), *Black Lives Matter: Poems for A New World* (2020) *Bollocks to Brexit: an Anthology of Poems and Short Fiction* (2019), and *Leicester 2084 AD: New Poems about The City* (2018), all published by CivicLeicester. He is the author of *The Gospel According to Bobba*.

Andy N is the author of nine full-length poetry books, the most recent being *From the Diabetic Ward Volume 1* and is the co-host of Chorlton Cum Hardy's always welcoming Spoken Word Open Mic night 'Speak Easy'. He also runs / co-runs podcasts such as Spoken Label, Reading in Bed, and Storytime with Andy and Amanda and does ambient music under the name of Ocean in a Bottle. His blog is: onewriterandhispc.blogspot.com

Nasrin Parvaz became a civil rights activist when the Islamic regime took power in 1979. She was arrested in 1982, and spent eight years in prison. her books are, *One Woman's Struggle in Iran: A Prison Memoir*, and *The Secret Letters from X to A* (Victorina Press, 2018) http://nasrinparvaz.org/

Leonie Philip is a mother, sister, and a grandmother. She started writing a long time ago. Her writing style varies according to her moods. She has experience of open mic reading. She loves to paint, knit bespoke dishcloths, and bake her own bread. She is an avid reader who also loves listening to audible. She hopes one day to publish her work and record them to music.

Natasha Polomski, a mature interdisciplinary student, writer and spoken word artist living in London.

Steve Pottinger is an engaging and accomplished performer who has performed at Ledbury and StAnza poetry festivals, at the Edinburgh Free Fringe, and in venues the length and breadth of the country. His sixth volume of poems, *thirty-one small acts of love and resistance* published by Ignite Books, is out now.

Matteo Preabianca is a multilingual expert in global education, languages teaching, training, translation and related methodologies. He has a PhD in global language education and has taught in universities in Australia and China. He also has extensive practical experience as a languages teacher, translator and writer in North America, Europe, Russia, Australia and Asia. He speaks Chinese (Mandarin) and English at an advanced level and is a native Italian speaker. In addition, he was appointed by the Italian Government's Ministry of Foreign Affairs to the General Council of Italians Abroad (CGIE), and specifically works in the Commission for Promoting the Italian Language Abroad. He is also a creative practitioner of music and sound art, a writer and a novelist. He practices and teaches Buddhism https://mattwhitestone.wixsite.com/mprea/

Munya Radzi is founder of Regularise, a migrant-founded and -led grassroots campaign group and collective which seeks to improve the quality of life of the estimated 600,000 to 1.2 million undocumented migrants living in the UK by attaining basic rights and a safer and more equitable path to settlement and citizenship

mona rae was inspired to write "After the Ofsted Visit" after attending the 2022 Burston School Strike Rally, commemorating the student-led strike against the dismissal of teachers Annie and Tom Higdon, who believed the power of learning as an instrument to create social justice. Their child-centred approach to education enthused students to express their opinions and feelings.

S Reeson is a multi-disciplined artist, who has suffered with anxiety and depression since childhood. They increasingly produce videos of their work for dissemination via YouTube. They came out as bisexual in their 40's. Their poetry has been published by The Poetry Society, Bloomsbury/One World, Flapjack Press, Dreich and Forest Arts plus many online indie journals, and they perform regularly in both virtual and IRL Open Mics.

Marilyn Ricci is a poet, playwright and editor. Her poetry has appeared in many small press magazines including *Magma*, *The Rialto* and *Modern Poetry in Translation*. Her pamphlet, *Rebuilding a Number 39*, was published by HappenStance Press and her first full collection, *Night Rider,* was published by SoundsWrite Press. Her latest poetry sequence, *Dancing At The Asylum*, is available from Quirky Press.

Kay Ritchie grew up in Glasgow and Edinburgh, lived in London, Spain and Portugal and worked as a freelance photographer and radio producer. Published in magazines and anthologies in the UK, Ireland and Africa, she has performed at events like Aye Write, Women's Aid Billion Women Rising & the Edinburgh Fringe. Her poems have appeared in an installation in

Glasgow's Pollock Park and a Historic Scotland film. She likes to walk and in 2019 walked the Portuguese coastal camino Santiago compostela. Next year she hopes to walk the Hebridean Way across ten Scottish islands.

Caroline Rooney is a writer and researcher who works in the area of African and Middle Eastern cultural studies. She grew up in Zimbabwe and lives in London.

Mandy Ross is a poet, playwright and children's author, gathering voices and stories in the city and in the green. Her song lyrics, "Human Journeys", were commissioned by Royal Liverpool Philharmonic Orchestra, and sung by over 10,000 children in 2022, in the Philharmonic Hall in Hope Street, Liverpool. Mandy has worked with Echo Eternal, BMAG, CBSO, interfaith groups, cancer patients and mental health service users. Her illustrated poetry picture book *Tree Whispers* was published by Child's Play International this year. As one half of Secret City Arts, Mandy works with storytellers, musicians, photographers and filmmakers to bring words off the page. She is also a qualified counsellor, combining creativity and wellbeing. www.mandyross.co.uk www.secretcityarts.com Twitter @MandyRoss111

Hastie Salih is originally from the Kurdish region in Northern Iraq and spent her childhood in Wales and Germany. She has published short stories and poems in Germany and Britain and works as a GP in Essex. She is a member of Exiled Ink. Her debut novel *Dahlia and Carys* was published in February 2023.

Chrys Salt MBE has performed across the UK and Europe, India, Australia, USA, Canada and Africa. She was International Poet at The Tasmanian Poetry Festival 2019. She has been recipient of awards and bursaries (various) and in 2014 was awarded an MBE in the Queen's Birthday Honours List for Services to The Arts.

Fran Sani was born in Vigevano, Italy, in 1995. He writes for the theatre and occasionally directs. He is currently conducting a PhD at De Montfort University, Leicester.

Barbara Saunders writes about social justice. Her work appears in anthologies such as *Ukraine In the Work of International Poets* (Literary Waves Publishing); *Poetry and Settled Status for All* (CivicLeicester); *Black Lives Matter:*

Poems for a New World (CivicLeicester); *Over Land Over Sea: Poems for those seeking refuge* (Five Leaves Publications) which is translated into Italian and Romanian; *A Farewell to Art: Chagall, Shakespeare and Prospero* (Ben Uri Gallery, 2018) as well as magazines such as The London Reader and The Journal.

Joel Scarfe is widely published. His poems feature internationally in magazines, anthologies and periodicals. He lives in Bristol with the Danish ceramicist Rebecca Edelmann and their two children.

Mahvash Shafiei was born in Shiraz, Iran and is a Law graduate, poet, writer, reporter and journalist in the field of environment and social issues. Besides writing poems and stories, she also works in theater. Due to political problems, she had to leave Iran and immigrate to France. In France, she has finished her fourth book, which is a novel, and is translating it into French. Her other book is poetry, which has been translated into English, but has not yet been successfully published. Her published works include: "A collection of Clarice stories" in 2010, Iran; the collection of poems, "A gun that does not shoot is dead" in 2020 in Iran, and "Undated" in Persian and French in 2022 in France. She also has articles and poems in reputable magazines and websites in Iran and abroad.

Sue Skyrme has been a political activist all her life and supported many human rights causes. She was a Radical Midwife and a keen cyclist who travelled the world. Sue has been a member of the Socialist Choir, Red Leicester since 1997, she wrote the lyrics "Get On Yer Bike" to the music of "Don't Fence Me In". The song is a humorous poke at the famous speech of Norman Tebbit, suggesting people get on their bikes to get a job. The song is a favourite of the choir and always generates a laugh when it is sung.

Sam Smith has been editor of *The Journal* (once 'of Contemporary Anglo-Scandinavian Poetry') for nigh on 30 years. Born Blackpool 1946 he now lives in Blaengarw, South Wales. Day jobs have included psychiatric nurse, residential social worker, milkman, plumber, laboratory analyst, groundsman, sailor, computer operator, scaffolder, gardener, painter & decorator... working at anything which paid the rent, enabled him to raise his three daughters and which didn't get too much in the way of his writing. He has a several novels and few poetry collections to his name - http://samsmithbooks.weebly.com & http://thesamsmith.webs.com His latest poetry collection is *Mirror, Mirror* erbacce-press

Born and raised by Hong Kong and the 21ˢᵗ century, **Jack So** is an actor, writer and performer with a love of astronomy and the neighbours' cat. The pandemic showed him a warm welcome to Britain indeed, and he has since found a second home in Manchester and its people. Jack has performed original writing with theatre companies such as Blue Balloon and Switch_Mcr. His poetry is featured in the Buzzin Bards Anthology 2021.

A P Staunton moved South in the great Liverpool exodus of the early 1980's when, as Margaret Thatcher's right hand man Lord Geoffrey Howe put it, the city was subjected to "managed decline." Another of Thatcher's henchmen, Sir Norman Tebbit advised the jobless and worthless to "get on their bikes" to find work. He did. It wasn't his bike. He's sorry. Worked on various building sites across Europe and southern England, often homeless in affluent towns and cities where the welcome was far from warm. At 60 he found the pen was lighter than the hod and has since won countless poetry slams, appeared at the Royal Albert Hall, Bestival and Port Eliot festivals and was recently on Sky Arts Life and Rhymes with Benjamin Zephaniah. He's even played The Pretty Bricks in Walsall. Who said beggars can't be choosers?

Tom Stockley is a multidisciplinary artist and writer working across the UK. They are proudly queer, gender non-conforming, neurodivergent and a descendant of working class Jewish refugees. They are interested in our human experience, collectively and as individuals, creating conversations around identity, culture, mental health and the places we call home.

Trefor Stockwell lives and works on the Isle of Anglesey, with occasional sessions at his flat in Moscow. He has a PhD in Creative writing from Bangor University and is currently engaged on a dystopian novel, a further volume of poetry and a collection of short stories reflecting life in Russia.

George Symonds blogs at www.guiltynation.wordpress.com. His grandmother Renata claimed asylum in the UK in the 1930s. If seeking refuge today in 2023, the UK authorities could detain (imprison) and threaten her with violent removal to Rwanda, amongst other indignities.

Sylvia Telfer is an international award-winning Scottish poet and short story writer frequently published in magazines, anthologies, etc. (e.g. Poetry

Review; Poetry Pen to Print 2019 Arts Council of England; 'Gutter 20', Scottish PEN's *Declarations on Freedom for Writers & Readers Anthology;* The San Francisco State University Review, etc.). BA (Hons) English, The University of London, is a qualified English teacher, and one of her jobs was In-House Publications Manager at the University of Hong Kong. She is a campaigner to halt climate change, a feminist, and an equal rights activist. She is proud and enriched to now have black folk within her family.

Pam Thompson is a writer and educator based in Leicester. Her publications include *The Japan Quiz* (Redbeck Press, 2009) and *Show Date and Time*, (Smith | Doorstop, 2006). Pam has a PhD in Creative Writing from De Montfort University and her second collection, *Strange Fashion*, was published by Pindrop Press in 2017. She is a Hawthornden Fellow and a Committee Member for Word!, a spoken-word night at Attenborough Arts Centre in Leicester.

Lauren Tormey is an American-born immigrant who moved to Scotland in 2011 and never left. Since she was granted Indefinite Leave to Remain in 2020, she has been campaigning for a more humane immigration system. Her poem describes one of the first experiences she had arriving at the UK border after getting Indefinite Leave to Remain. This experience was a factor in her decision to apply for British citizenship, which she was granted in 2023.

Deborah Tyler-Bennett is a European writer who has work published in a variety of new anthologies and journals, as well as having had eight volumes of poetry and three of linked short stories published. In 2021 she won the adult section of Writing East Midlands'/ Derbyshire Wildlife Trust's Ghosts of the Landscape Competition with her poem "The Ash Woman Speaks". New work has dealt with themes of ecology, folklore, and those perceived as being on society's margins.

Elizabeth Uter is a double award-winning short story writer, winning *Home Croydon City Of Stories* Competition in 2022 and *Brent City of Stories* in 2017. She is also an award-winning poet, winning the 2018 Poem for Slough Competition in two categories. She's facilitated Farrago Poetry workshops; performed at the prestigious Queen's Park Literary Festival, London. Published works include: *Bollocks To Brexit: An Anthology of Poems and Short Fiction* (CivicLeicester), *Reach Magazine Issues 249 & 252* (Indigo Dreams

Publishing), *Sarasvati Magazines Issue 055* (Indigo Dreams Publishing), *2020 & 2021 Writing From Inlandia* (Inlandia Institute), *This Is Our Place: A Nature Anthology* (Spread The Word), *Nature, Framed: An Anthology of Nature Writing,* (London Wildlife Trust with Great North Wood and National Lottery through Arts Council England), *I Give My Word: An Anthology of Writing from* Open Book (Open Book), *Echoes, An Anthology Volume 2* (Writerz and Scibez CIC), *Womanhood Anthology* (Shakti Women In The Community), *Other Lives in Samuel Pepys's Diary: A Collection of Creative Writing inspired by Pepys's Journal of the 1660s* (PEPYSHistory, Reimagining the Restoration) (University of Leicester).

Michael Walling is Artistic Director of Border Crossings, Director of the ORIGINS Festival, & Visiting Professor at Rose Bruford College. He has directed numerous productions across four continents, winning awards for TWO GENTLEMEN OF VERONA in the US & PAUL & VIRGINIE in Mauritius. Opera includes THE RING (ENO).

Matthew James Wiegel is a Dene and Métis poet & artist born & raised in Edmonton. Currently pursuing a PhD in English at the University of Alberta, he holds a Bachelor of Science in Biological Sciences. He is the designer for Moon Jelly House press & his words & art have been published by people like Arc Poetry Magazine, Book*Hug, The Polyglot, &The Mamawi Project. Matthew is a National Magazine Award finalist, Nelson Ball Prize finalist, Cécile E. Mactaggart award winner, & winner of both the 2020 Vallum Chapbook Award & 2021 Nichol Chapbook Award for his chapbook "It Was Treaty / It Was Me". His debut full-length collection "Whitemud Walking" recently won the Alcuin Society Award for book design, & is available now from Coach House Books. Matthew was part of ORIGINS Writers in 2021.

Michele Witthaus is based in the UK. Her writing has appeared in a number of anthologies and other publications and her pamphlet, 'From a Sheltered Place', was published in August 2020 by Wild Pressed Books. She is the 2020 winner of Leicester Writers' Club's Ena Young Award for Poetry.

Gregory Woods is emeritus professor of gay and lesbian studies at Nottingham Trent University. Six of his poetry collections have been published by Carcanet Press, the latest being *Records of an Incitement to Silence* (2021). His cultural histories include *Articulate Flesh: Male Homo-*

eroticism and Modern Poetry (1987), *A History of Gay Literature* (1998), and *Homintern: How Gay Culture Liberated the Modern World* (2017), all from Yale University Press. www.gregorywoods.co.uk

Nina Worthington is a Principal Research Fellow at the Sidney De Haan Research Centre for Arts and Health, Canterbury Christ Church University. She completed a PhD at Liverpool Hope University exploring lived experiences of disability in theatres across England. Previous degrees include a BA in Drama from Newman University and MRes in Directing from University of Birmingham. Nina is based in the West Midlands and has over 16-years' experience working in arts and media organisations, creating radio, film, and live performances. Her work is shaped by a passion to shift disability perceptions, impact progress towards more equitable arts practices, and her personal experiences parenting children with physical and language impairments.

Neelam Wright is a UK independent Indian film scholar. She also has an active role in equality, diversity and inclusion – specifically supporting minority ethnic staff and researchers and looking at Decolonisation in the Higher Education context.

Trevor Wright is a trainer and consultant specialising in neurodiversity and a Derby-based poet and co-founder of the annual Derby Poetry Festival, established in 2017. He has performed at many local poetry events as well as the Nottingham and Gloucester Poetry Festivals and Edinburgh Fringe. He has been a commissioned writer on the Writing East Midlands Local: Vocal former coalfields project, with older people's mental health on the Elder Tree initiative and with Writing East Midlands, set up the Beyond the Spectrum creative writing for autistic people project. His work has featured in several anthologies including *Welcome to Leicester* (Dahlia), *Nottingham* (Dostoyevsky Wannabe), *Over Land Over Sea* (Five Leaves Press), *World Jam Us v Covid* (Beam Editions). He has two poetry collections, *Outsider Heart* and *Salt Flow* published by Nottingham's Big White Shed. Trevor is also a Writer Trustee of the Nottingham UNESCO City of Literature and a Fellow of the Royal Society of Arts.

Duaa Zahida loves art and painting. She is studying for a degree in biology and works with three charities that support people in need.

Kathy Zwick has taught History and Social Studies in international schools in Belgium, Iran, and the UK for over 25 years. New and flexible perspectives are now more important than ever and should be a part of every school curriculum. Many of her poems recycle ideas from favourite old lesson plans.

Acknowledgements

Acknowledgements and thanks to all who distributed our call for submissions, and to all who responded.

The cover image, "The New Union Flag" is an art project by the socially engaged artist Gil Mualem-Doron. Launched in late 2014, the project re-imagines the Union Jack and celebrates the communities contributing to the UK's cultural legacy. Re-created with traditional fabric designs representing various British communities, the New Union Flag transforms the traditional Union Jack from an archetype of uniformity into a dynamic and celebratory performance of diversity.

Some of the poems in this anthology have been published previously as follows –

"Haiku" by Helen Buckingham, in the journal, *Blithe Spirit*, Volume 32 Issue 1, 2022

"Europium" by Philip Burton, in *Gaia Warnings* (Palewell Press, 2017)

"Welcome Back to Britain: The Veteran's Return" by Richard Byrt (with the title, "Two Bags, Two Voices", a change of date in the second part and most of the commentary in the footnote), in: North, J. and Taylor, J. (eds.) *Writing Lives Together. An Anthology of Poetry and Prose* (University of Leicester Centre for New Writing, 2017)

"Uncle Henry", by David Clark, in *Second Generation Voices*, the magazine run by Second Generation Network, based in London, Issue 55, January 2014, p.10

"Unreadable" by A C Clarke, in the magazine, The Poets' Republic

"The Flag of my Britain has More than Three Colours" by Cardinal Cox, in *Small Word: Wide World* (Allographic Press, 2019)

"Whiteness" by Heaven Crawley, on The artist and the prof (16 July 2020) https://theartistandtheprof.art.blog/2020/07/16/whiteness

"Engelestân" by Kimia Etemadi, an earlier version, in the print edition of *The Other Side of Hope* https://othersideofhope.com/index.html

"Kings Heath Park" by Corinne Fowler, in Corinne Fowler, 2020, *Green Unpleasant Land: Creative Responses to Rural England's Colonial Connections* (Leeds: Peepal Tree Press)

"Cotswolds" by Corinne Fowler, in Corinne Fowler, 2020, *Green Unpleasant Land: Creative Responses to Rural England's Colonial Connections* (Leeds: Peepal Tree Press)

"Myrtilla" by Corinne Fowler, in Corinne Fowler, 2020, *Green Unpleasant Land: Creative Responses to Rural England's Colonial Connections* (Leeds: Peepal Tree Press)

"Into the Home Office, 10AM" by Charles G Lauder, Jr, in *Dreich*, Volume 4, Number 2, 2022

"Approaching Britain, Snapshots 2017" by Helen Moore, in *Molly Bloom,* 2021

"Pointless Packaging" by Chris Morley, is among the repertoire of songs the Red Leicester Choir regularly performs on the streets of Leicester and at events around the city and beyond https://youtu.be/1a2fU9XAYpc

"What A Wonderful War" by Ambrose Musiyiwa, in *The Morning Star*, 5 January 2023 https://www.morningstaronline.co.uk/article/c/21st-century-poetry-what-wonderful-war

"Swallows" by steve pottinger, in steve pottinger, 2017, *A fine fine place* (Ignite Books)

"Moving on" by steve pottinger, in steve pottinger, 2017, *A fine fine place* (Ignite Books)

"England" by steve pottinger, in steve pottinger, 2017, *A fine fine place* (Ignite Books)

"Get On Yer Bike" by Sue Skyrme and Chris Morley, is among the repertoire of songs the Red Leicester Choir regularly performs on the streets of Leicester and at events around the city and beyond https://youtu.be/O3RvHpTK5Ng

"Hummus on Matzo" by Tom Stockley, in the magazine, *All My Relations* (ed. Chris Talbot-Heindl, nat raum, and tommy blake, Forthcoming)

"Who are we now to welcome you?" and "On this land also" by Michael Walling, and "I found my body yesterday" by Matthew James Wiegel, were originally written for REMEMBRANCES, a performance piece by Border Crossings, AVA Dance Company and b.solomon//ELECTRIC MOOSE, commissioned by Birmingham 2022. The performance sought to question the idea of the Commonwealth and of welcoming, particularly in relation to Indigenous people, who have such strong protocols around welcome: https://www.bordercrossings.org.uk/whats-on/programme/remembrances

Printed in Great Britain
by Amazon

23666091R00129